BRAND YOUR OWN BUSINESS

A GUIDEBOOK TO
BUILDING YOUR OWN BRAND

TIM MILES

WITH
RYAN PATRICK &
LYNN MILES PEISKER

TABLE 49

PRESS

To order copies, visit timmilesco.com or call 615-538-5511.

Cover design by Caleb Agee, Carrie Waller, and the BYOB VIP Team

Authors' Photographs by Karyl Wackerlin

Rad Awesome Boss Name for Tim's Thing by Tim Robinson

Special Thanks to Jason Wetherholt for inviting us to breakfast at OPH.

Special Thanks to John Miles, Laura Rickheim, Mallory Jensen, Michele Miller, Nancy Schneider, Garrison Cox, Eric Anderson, Julie Hein, Garrison Cox again, Tina Johnson, Laura McCallum, Denise McIntosh, Garrison Cox another time, Lisa Wise, Jeff Sexton, Carrie Waller, Jessica Porter, and the rest of our amazing BYOB-VIP Team. We are grateful for your smarts!

SECTIONS

On July 12, 2012, the preview copies of my first book arrived while we were visiting my parents' home in Gifford, Illinois. We were chatting about it in the kitchen when I noticed Dad had disappeared. He snuck off to the living room to be the first to read what would go on to become a bestseller. Pop, what I wouldn't give to have you here to read this one. I hope we made you proud.

This book is dedicated to Rich Miles, 1936-2016, and to Janet Miles, who cared for her husband of 56 years with the same grace, class, and love with which she continues to care for her children, grandchildren, friends, farmers, and family.

We love you, Mom. We miss you, Dad.

This book would also not be possible if not for God, Deidre, Julie, and John.

COMPANY EXERCISE: YOUR DEDICATION

A powerful transaction takes place in your heart and mind when you:

(A) Make things personal.

(B) Sign your name.

Below, you're going to do both. For whom are you doing this? I want you to choose someone specific for whom you're going to make the effort to not only read but complete the exercises in this book. Choose an employee. Choose a family member. Choose a parent, pastor, or now-deceased mentor. Raise the stakes and refer back to this page when you feel like you're losing steam.

I, _____, will read this book and

complete its exercises not only for myself but also for

_____ because _____

_____

_____

_____

_____

_____

_____

_____
Signature

_____
Date

PREFACE

I DON'T BELIEVE IN SMALL BUSINESS.

Every night, for at least a few minutes (and sometimes for hours), I lie awake in bed thinking about the people who work for our company in some capacity. Do you know what I'm talking about?

So many in the media would consider my company a "small" business... I suspect anyone who uses that term has never owned one.

It doesn't keep me awake at night because it's small. It keeps me awake at night because it's huge. It's massive. At times, it feels like my whole world.

Know what I mean? How dare someone else refer to my business as "small." I reject the premise of "small."

But I believe with all my heart and soul that the secret to strong communities—whether local or global—is strong, sustainable, gracefully growing family businesses.

If you've ever lain awake at night worried about your family or the families of those people who work for or with you, this book is for you.

If you've ever felt things were moving too fast with too many choices or you just weren't sure you could find a way to do a little bit more with a little bit less, this book is for you.

If you own or work for one of the approximately 7.77 million family-owned businesses in the United States and Canada, this book is for you... written by one of you.

IT DOESN'T KEEP ME AWAKE AT NIGHT BECAUSE IT'S SMALL. IT KEEPS ME AWAKE AT NIGHT BECAUSE IT'S HUGE. IT'S MASSIVE. AT TIMES, IT FEELS LIKE MY WHOLE WORLD.

It's the best possible time to be alive...

when everything you thought you knew is wrong.

TOM STOPPARD

SECTION ZERO

RECALIBRATION

GET ONE THING STRAIGHT

Your plumbing company is not in the plumbing business.

Your restaurant is not in the food business.

Your hotel is not in the hospitality business.

Your school is not in the education business.

Your company is in the service business, and everyone in your company is in the marketing department.

And if everyone—everyone—in your company doesn't have that straight, then nothing else matters.

And if you, personally, don't understand that you're serving whomever is below you (not above you) on the org chart, then nothing else matters. By serving those "below" you, you automatically serve those "above" you.

Think about that for five minutes, then think about sharing it with your company.

One... Two... Three... Four... Five...

Then please proceed with being awesome. Thank you.

"WHAT'S MARKETING, DADDY?"

"Daddy, this package says 'World Beater.' Can you beat the world with these spikes?"

A few years back, I took my then eight-year-old son, Will, with me to return some golf spikes.

"Not really, buddy," I say.

"So, it's a lie?"

"Well, Will. It's marketing," I reply.

"What's marketing, Daddy?"

I explain, "Well, Will, the company that makes those spikes uses certain words—like "World Beater"—to make you pick their spikes over the other spikes at the store."

"But you can't reeeeeally beat the world with them, right Daddy?" Will asks.

"No, buddy."

Will thinks. "So, it's a lie."

Can you argue with that?

If you can't fool an eight-year-old (granted, a shockingly brilliant one), what makes you think you can fool the rest of us?

THAT GUY

You know That Guy.

The one who wants to be the center of attention at every party.

The braggart who one-ups everyone in the room.

The jerk who spends the whole night talking about himself.

You know That Guy, right?

You go out of your way to avoid That Guy.

You certainly don't want to BE That Guy.

So why do you become That Guy in your advertising?

"We have the best selection!"

"Nobody can beat our price!"

"Award-winning service!"

"We're the tri-state sales leader!"

"We won't be undersold!"

"You've tried the rest, now buy from the best!"

Who cares?

Your customers don't want to listen to you talk about you. They want you to explain how you can help them...

Save time

Save money

Look better

Be healthier

Lose weight

Stay regular

Get out of debt

Start a family

Stay comfortable

Build muscle

Attain wealth

Get rid of their junk

Improve their portfolio

Find their soulmate

Buy their dream home

Forget their problems

Keep their family safe

Can you help? Don't brag. Tell. Then, do.

Do it so well that others want to brag about you.

That's how you go from being That Guy to being THE Guy.

WHO OR WHAT, THEN, SHOULD BE THE SUBJECT OF YOUR MARKETING?

You? Your product? Your service? Nope. Your customer.

Once you make your customer—or potential customer—the focus of your marketing, you begin to look at everything differently.

Because everything—as playwright Tom Stoppard said in the heading of this section—you thought you knew is wrong.

And yet, you already have everything you need inside you to tackle this brave new world. In a stroke of accidental magic, I scribbled the secret down on a napkin a while back...

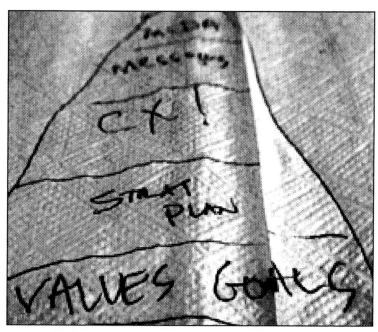

The Bacon Pancake-Fueled Sketch that Started It All

"I THINK WE'VE GOT SOMETHING SPECIAL HERE..."

Like so many good things, it was born out of pancakes and bacon.

It started as a way to prove my point to the leaders of a church group that we were giving some pro bono marketing help to. They were concerned about their message. Over breakfast, I invited them to think more deeply about their purpose and values before they considered their message.

To explain my point, I drew a pyramid on a napkin. A few hours later, it occurred to me that the drawing could be used to make the same point to other clients and help them do the thinking that must precede effective message development.

It also occurred to me that I might have created something that could help every other owner-operated company and non-profit in the world.

I realize that's a lot to say about a pyramid. Maybe I'm nuts. I'm probably nuts.

But... It's simple to explain. It's simple to understand. It's simple (for our company) to use. And it's true.

Like many profound truths, yes, it's simple. but that doesn't mean it's easy. We call it The First Order Of Business.

Are you ready to turn the page on your marketing?

WHAT IS THE FIRST ORDER OF BUSINESS?

The First Order of Business is a framework which categorizes and prioritizes communication, branding, and marketing for any owner-operated company or nonprofit organization. It's also the tool our company uses to diagnose and treat problems for businesses around the world.

But, more than that, it shows our clients what deserves the highest priority in their marketing, and in fact, what's got to come first, second, third, fourth, and fifth for any business to be successful.

Millions of companies get it wrong. Tens of thousands of vendors that profit from those millions of companies aren't asking questions deep enough to really help them.

Until you know your goals and values, you cannot come up with a strategic plan. Your strategic plan—based on those goals and values—dictates how you treat the customer (including your most important customers: your employees). Your values, your goals, your plan, and your customer experience determine your message.

Once you've got a solid structure of values, goals, a strategic plan, a delightful customer experience, and a strong message, you can begin thinking about choosing media channels.

Throughout the world, people have this turned upside down. Companies invest hundreds of billions of dollars and pounds and euros and yuan and yen and rupees into message development and media buying and placement. What thought do those companies—and what thought are you—giving to build a strong foundation to support those investments?

Throughout this book, we're going to share the research and successes that have helped our clients use it to not only survive but thrive.

If you're willing to do the work, The First Order Of Business framework can help you do the same.

THE FIRST ORDER OF BUSINESS

THE ROADMAP TO BRANDING YOUR OWN BUSINESS

At the end of this book, you'll have

- a profound understanding of how the world of communication in business has changed (and how it hasn't)

- a crystal-clear vision of what you're trying to make happen and what's in your way

- short-term, measurable goals to overcome the obstacles preventing you from completing your mission

- a Brand Diamond consisting of five core values that shape how your company thinks, acts, and sees the world

- a Company Constitution declaring your values and beliefs as observable systems, policies, and procedures

- a fully mapped and tuned Customer Experience embedding your core values and the 14 facets of Shareworthy Customer Service

- a Copy Right style guide to simplify and give consistency to your messaging strategy

- a new way to think about a message calendar and a better understanding of why you should use it to create more ads more often

- a formula for writing any piece of persuasive copy

- comprehension of the three kinds of three kinds of media (not a typo)—how they're changing, how to evaluate them, and how to make an impact in each

- confidence and belief in how all these things work together to raise your signal above the noise

- buy-in and assistance from your team to help you accomplish your mission

It's hard to believe, right? It's hard to fathom one book could so radically change your compete philosophy on marketing.

First, I bet it reinforces many of the things you intuitively believe to be true.

Second, breathe.

RELAX. YOU'VE GOT THIS.

Yes, it's scary. If you own a family business, there have never been more people trying to help you spend your marketing budget. More channels. More choices. More noise. And while there are many fine, noble, well-intentioned people out there, it's simple math to conclude there are more snakes, weasels, and magic bean and bullet peddlers as well.

This book contains a series of ascending, connected levels to show you exactly how we've helped hundreds of family businesses and thousands of people understand it's within them to not only survive but thrive. It's within you, too. Not unlike Dorothy and her friends in *The Wizard of Oz*, you've had everything you need inside you all along.

We wrote this book to give you belief, confidence, and reassurance that, if you're willing to do the work, you know what you believe, and you have the conviction of those beliefs, then you can navigate this scary age of change... simply by being you.

There's never been a better time to do what it is you do, but there's also never been a more important time to be good at what it is you do. Are you ready? Awesome.

But before we get started, I want to welcome you to a new age.

WELCOME TO THE AGE OF RAPID DISTRACTION

"These sure are exciting times, aren't they?"

That's what people say, isn't it? When, often what they mean instead is:

"These sure are uncertain times, aren't they?"

... or ...

"These sure are freakin' scary times, aren't they?!?"

Hogwash, I tell you. These are exciting times. The coming year promises to be filled with success and adventure for leaders of companies who keep their wits about them, and who are ready to swing the hammer and take action.

That said, there's never been a more frightening time to be average at or indifferent about what you do. You have to change. You know the alternative, don't you?

Sure, life was simpler back then... for you. To paraphrase the late British playwright Douglas Adams, it's normal for those being born into it and exciting for young people trying to get a job in it.

For you, again paraphrasing Adams, it may very well be against the natural order of things.

It seems like five minutes ago when you could turn on your radio or switch between your three television stations and be perfectly content!

You could walk out to your mailbox and get your handful of daily mail. The only SPAM we knew came in a spiffy little tin.

Unsure who to call? Grab the Yellow Pages.

And now, day after day, we wake up with more choices, more options, more channels, and more noise.

Things are busier, but are they better?

Sorry to say I'm not certain that's the right question.

I'm not sure it's helpful or particularly relevant to bury your head in the sand, mumble about the past and long for simpler, sweeter times.

Perhaps it's best instead, don't you think, to rise up into the *Finding Nemo*-esqe slipstream and ride the current into the future?

Want some good news? It's never been simpler.

Please don't confuse simple with easy. Simple simply means getting your thinking clear. Once you have clarity, you'll be able to amplify your signal above the noise and do far more with less than at any other time in the history of your company.

THERE'S NEVER BEEN A BETTER TIME FOR YOU TO TRANSFORM YOUR COMPANY'S COMMUNICATIONS PLAN AND MARKETING BUDGET.

So, let's recap: A number of companies are poised to grab market share in the coming years without necessarily infusing their marketing budgets with huge wads of cash. But each of these companies has a rather similar set of defining characteristics:

- They're good at what they do

- They like talking about what they do

- They don't use economic uncertainty and consumer credit instability as excuses to pull an eeyore and go all "woe-is-me"

- They're not trying to drive using the rear-view mirror... They're looking ahead with eyes wide open

- They have a plan

That last one's important.

One of the natural side effects of our recent explosion in technology is the sheer heft of voices and choices hurtling toward us. The last time market research firm Yankelovich did their advertising bombardment study, they found the average person living in a city saw as many as 5,000 messages per day. That was waaaaay back in 2007! Imagine how many ads you collide with today!

According to AT&T, the average teenage girl in America sends and receives more than 4,000 text messages each month. According to Gallup, disengaged workers cost American companies more than $500,000,000,000 in lost productivity last year!

We are the most distracted population in the history of the earth. How can you plan to rise above the noise?

Let me give you three ways. I learned them from an eccentric futurist to whom I'll introduce you at the end of the next section.

1. Frequency

Imagine a woman calling you—madder than heck—and accusing you of false advertising. Then, you come to find out, she uses your product intended for daily use only every other week but expects the results to be delivered all the time.

She isn't using as directed, is she?

Whatever tools and tactics you choose to include in your marketing plan—and that's really a different subject for a different day—you should plan to deliver your message to consumers for as long as you plan to be in business.

Customers and potential customers have this annoying habit of caring about things *they think are important* rather than what *we think should be important to them.* We're all too busy, we're all too alternately focused and distracted, we're all too over-communicated, unless you tell us and then keep on telling us.

When you understand that you need to be there—in their world—a little bit each week for the rest of your business' life, you begin to understand the degree to which you must scale your commitment.

Whatever your medium. Whatever your message. Use as directed.

2. Consistency

Do your messages—again, regardless of medium—have the same look, say, and feel?

We're talking about word choice, pacing, white space, fonts, music and audio signatures, and so on.

Though every President or Prime Minister has a team of speech writers, their mission is singular: to write in the distinctive voice of the leader. The same should be true for all your messaging.

Do they contain certain repetitious elements that allow these super-busy, back-button, over-communicated consumers to easily connect the dots from one of your messages to the next?

Our team first helps our clients develop style guides that assemble—consciously—the defining characteristics of a message plan.

Your elements should fit your business naturally and authentically so that there is no disconnect when a consumer chooses to do business with you. Of course, your marketing messages should contain these elements for as long as you intend to be in business.

3. Relevance

Most critically—given our time and attention deficiencies—are you talking to consumers about what matters to consumers in a language consumers understand?

Time and again I've seen business owners who try and convince me that if the consumer only understood the nuance and intricacies of what they were selling, they'd for sure do business with them every time.

But consumers don't want to understand. As I said before, consumers have this nagging habit of caring about their own lives, their own worlds.

You're the invader here. You're the interrupter. You'd better dadgum-well make it relevant to me, and you'd better do it quickly.

Talk to consumers about what matters to consumers in a language consumers understand.

Doing so is easier than you might suspect. Ask them. Ask your customers! In his magnificent book on customer service, *Customers for Life*, automotive legend Carl Sewell said intuitively he knew customers knew better, but he "wasn't sure why. So we started asking customers what they didn't like about doing business with us, and they told us, quite often without mincing words." Mr. Sewell knew, and deep down you know, too. Follow Mr. Sewell's advice: "I started thinking about our company from the customers' point of view."

How to Use These Three Tools

Armed with those three tools, you can move forward fiercely into this undiscovered country, ready to gobble market share, whether it be by using web video or local search or radio or print or hiring a bi-plane with a banner... or a combination of them all.

Oh, and the eccentric futurist? Get this: he was a scientist who evidently rubbed meat paste onto the tongue of a dog over and over again. Every time he did it, he rang a bell. Over and over he repeated this process: meat paste, bell, meat paste, bell, meat paste, bell. Word on the street is that suddenly this dog started drooling when he heard the bell.

Crazy, huh? And for his little experiment in frequency, consistency, and relevance, they gave Ivan Pavlov the Nobel Prize for his research into conditioned response... in 1904.

THE DIFFERENCE BETWEEN MARKETING & ADVERTISING

As a general rule, as you continue to grow your company, your marketing budget will—or should—continue to increase as a percentage of revenue.

But there's a difference between marketing and advertising. We define "marketing" as every touchpoint you have with a customer. What's a touchpoint? Any possible interaction your company has with potential customers. Business cards? Yep, that's a touchpoint. Your receptionist answering the phone, your trade show booth, your pay-per-click (PPC) ad campaign, and your service trucks are all examples of touchpoints. They also include:

- The cleanliness of your parking lot and your restrooms

- The lighting inside your store

- How well you keep your promises

- Your content marketing

- How well you speak to accurately perceived needs of customers

ONE COMPONENT OF

MARKETING IS ADVERTISING.

We define "advertising" as any message you pay money to place and run. Those messages you see in the sidebar of your Facebook wall? Someone paid to put those there. Those are advertising.

The way a customer raved on Facebook about the awesome experience she had with your company? That delightful, shareworthy experience is marketing.

And in spite of the fact that mass media is losing some of its mass, marketing—including its subset called advertising—continues to work.

In fact, with so many voices screaming for attention like an overcrowded preschool classroom, telling a great story—great marketing—has never been more important. The web tends to make good marketing for a good business work more quickly.

For unremarkable companies, advertising—PPC, Groupon, throwing stuff onto a TV or a radio, putting ads in mailboxes (whether email or old-fashioned)—is working less and less well by the second.

But a great company? Thanks to the lightning speed of interconnectivity, marketing and advertising can accelerate the growth of a great company exponentially.

Boom! A great company takes off because its great marketing and advertising are telling stories to prospects that make them want to be new customers. Those same stories also remind current customers of how awesome it is to do business—and how smart they are for doing business—with the company.

Have you ever been to Disney? They understand that every employee or cast member is in the marketing department. Every cast member has it branded into their brain that every touchpoint matters.

The same needs to be true of your employees and your company... whether you want to believe it or not.

IN THE WORKBOOK VERSION OF BRAND YOUR OWN BUSINESS, WE PROVIDE DOZENS OF EXERCISES AND WORKSHEETS TO WALK YOU THROUGH OUR METHODOLOGY. THE NEXT TWO PAGES FEATURE AN EXAMPLE OF ONE OF THE EXERCISES.

TO ORDER OR LEARN MORE ABOUT THE BYOB WORKBOOK, VISIT:

BRANDYOUROWN.BUSINESS

COMPANY EXERCISE: IDENTIFY TOUCHPOINTS

This exercise is for you and your team to identify the opportunities you have to touch potential and current customers.

Gather your team members to help with this exercise. Divide your team into similar-sized groups. Be sure to mix departments so that office and tech staff are not all together.

Have each group take 15 minutes to brainstorm and list touchpoints. Define touchpoints as any interaction your company has with someone. Give a few examples such as your website, invoices, hours on the door, staff tees, Christmas gifts, on-hold messaging, etc.

Have each group share its list and designate a person to record them on a master list as you discuss them.

Identify As Many Company Touchpoints As You Can.

You Have 15 Minutes!

_____

_____

_____

_____

_____

_____

_____

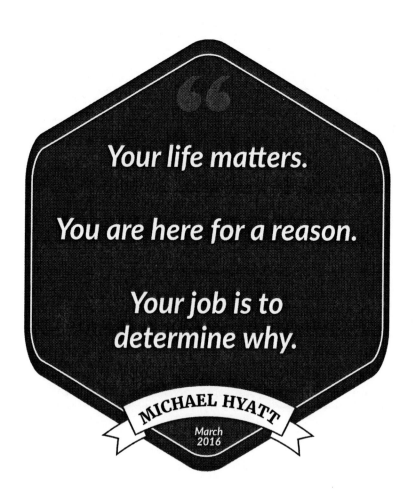

Your life matters.

You are here for a reason.

Your job is to
determine why.

MICHAEL HYATT

March
2016

SECTION ONE

GOALS & VALUES

WHAT IS IT, SPECIFICALLY, WHAT ARE YOU TRYING TO MAKE HAPPEN?

Can you tell me with such brevity and clarity that my seven-year-old (admittedly brilliant) daughter can understand? If you can't do that, how can you lead your team? Where are you leading them? Seriously.

If you have more than one goal, have you prioritized them? What if two of your goals come into conflict? Which one has priority?

What does your company stand for? What does your company stand against? What are the non-negotiable standards and values by which you make decisions and establish your systems, policies, and procedures?

Does your team know these things? Do they agree with them? If I asked them the same questions, would their answers mirror yours? They'd better.

Because in this Age of Rapid Distraction, it's going to take a focused team working together with shared values carrying them toward that celebration of your success.

Imagine gathering your team and popping champagne corks to celebrate. What are you celebrating? If you don't know—and if your team doesn't know and agree—you really shouldn't spend another dollar on marketing until you do. You're probably just throwing it away, and you worked hard for it!

HOW TO GET 20/20 VISION

At the end of the sub-section about goals, you're going to do a series of exercises to make sure your team is on the same page as they work toward your vision.

As you read through the next few pages, you'll understand why they're more necessary than ever.

We've refined these exercises over the years to help our clients visualize (and communicate) not only what it is they're trying to make happen, but also how to get started and subsequently enjoy the thrill of momentum.

Specifically, it's a 20/2/0 vision: A 20-year vision, with a two-year plan, can get you to Day Zero.

Day Zero? That's today.

Let's look ahead a little bit before we get to work.

THE 20-YEAR QUESTION

"Where do you see this company in 20 years? Where do you want it to be?"

It's all too easy to get caught up in the day-to-day activities of the business without pushing the pause button to consider the bigger picture.

It's a little like parenting. We get so busy with the urgent that the important can be overlooked. Keeping little people happy, safe, and healthy can consume all the energy in the household, leaving nothing left for casting a vision for the future.

The same is true for business—answering calls, staff turnover, sales projections, bids to prepare, work to get done—the daily urgencies cloud our long-term vision.

What do you want your owner-operated business to look like when it's all grown up?

Give it 20 years.

- Do you want a business you can sell to fund your retirement?

- Do you want to be ready to offer public shares?

- Do you want to build a business that you can pass on to your children to run? (This is the case for nearly all our current clients. It's also the case for our own business.)

- Do you want to live comfortably, make good investments, and simply close the doors when you are done?

There are no right or wrong answers to the 20-year question.

The only wrong answer is no answer, because if you don't know where you are going, how on earth will you ever get there?

The 20-year dream of our company has now been hashed out, talked over and sketched out on a piece of ripped and crooked spiral notebook paper. It's been scrawled with an ink pen with lines that squiggle on the page a bit. A couple of additional items have been added on, and an idea or two has been scratched out. A few names of second generation candidates have been bandied about. But they need to finish school first. We don't have all the specifics, but we know the framework. We know what our business will look like when it grows up.

All that's left is the 20 years of diet and exercise—also known as working the plan. But we're lucky, because unlike my current fitness plan, the food is delicious and the workout exhilarating.

ESTABLISH A BASELINE BY ASKING YOUR TEAM ONE ANONYMOUS QUESTION

Giving them a deadline of 72 hours, use Survey Monkey or another online survey service to allow your employees to answer the following question anonymously (with the accompanying description underneath it):

"WHAT IS IT, SPECIFICALLY,

YOU BELIEVE OUR COMPANY IS

TRYING TO MAKE HAPPEN?"

In the description below the question, write: "See it clearly in your mind. Say it clearly in your answer. Be specific. What do you understand to be our company's thing we're trying to make happen?"

What's more? Will they answer from a company's perspective: "We're trying to grow from $10mm in sales to $15mm in sales." Or will it be from a customer's perspective? "We're trying to make sure customers have a healthy alternative for their family to eat for dinner that's delivered directly to their home."

Will their answers be short-term visions or long-term?

How does preparing for this exercise make you feel? Excited? Nervous?

What does that feeling tell you about yourself?

Why are you asking them? Because we need to set a baseline of how aligned your own goal/mission is with your team's. We're also baby-stepping you into the idea of getting assessments and input from your team.

SURE, BIG GOALS ARE SCARY, BUT THEY'RE A GOOD SCARY

The biggest goals scare you the most, and they're the ones you know are worth doing.

They are the goals you can't do alone. They make you rely on your team.

They are the goals that seem too big to achieve. You will achieve them only one step at a time.

They are the goals that will change your current reality. So you step out in faith.

Recently I had the opportunity to hunker down and talk goals. Big goals. With people I love and respect. We weren't wimps about it. We were brave and bold.

Are we foolish to believe we can accomplish goals that big? Time will tell, but I think not. I think if we stay focused, accountable to one another, and prayerful, we can OWN THEM.

What are your biggest goals? If they seem a little (or a lot) scary, then you know you are on the right track.

WHAT IF A TEAM MEMBER'S VISIONS DO—OR DON'T—MATCH YOUR OWN?

No one said sitting in your chair was easy, did they? As an employer, how do you give feedback to your employees? Feedback is important, and so also, is the manner in which it is delivered.

It's time to make an invitation—because, remember, your surveys were anonymous—for people to find new work.

Invite dissenting opinions to privately contact you—not HR, you—and bravely step forward because you want to hear them out.

Then, schedule a time to hear them out. Then hear them out.

Maybe they'll help you identify a blind spot you and the rest of your team missed.

Maybe she's the right person, but she's in the wrong seat.

But, more than likely, they simply don't share your vision, and you've both got a choice to make:

Should you part ways or carry on like it never happened?

Wait... that's not really even a choice is it?

You must—MUST—have a team moving forward fiercely in the same direction to succeed in this age of rapid distraction.

If he or she has been a good team member, prepare for his or her separation with a classy letter of recommendation, but prepare.

6 STEPS TO SET & ACCOMPLISH GOALS TOWARD YOUR VISION

Your entire company now knows your mission and why it's important to you, and now you need a map to the treasure that is your successful future.

Goal setting is simple. That doesn't mean it's easy. Follow these tested steps:

1. What are the most important things we can do to improve our company to help us succeed in our mission? Once again, tell me in clear, concrete language. Use no more than three sentences my daughter could understand.

2. For each of the important things you listed in number one, what's in your way? Tell me what's holding you back. Some of these limiting factors will be known to you. Some won't. Blind spots can trip up anyone. It helps to have an outside eye, ear, and heart.

3. Once we know what to do, what are we going to do first, second, third? Multi-tasking is a myth that makes you dumber and less efficient. Prioritize the stuff you're trying to make happen. Delegate.

4. Brainstorm. Don't let this trip you up. What if money were no object? How would you solve your problem? Look outside your own business category. Has the HVAC industry already solved a similar problem? What about the amusement park industry? Review the previous chapter.

5. Do stuff. Go hard in the paint. Work your list.

6. Review and celebrate your progress with your team.

Again, we recommend asking your team for help. Use a tool like online survey software. Learn of blind spots and unleveraged assets, yes. But more importantly you'll earn their trust and buy-in because you're letting their voices be heard as you chart your course.

IN THE WORKBOOK VERSION OF
BRAND YOUR OWN BUSINESS,
WE PROVIDE 26 PAGES OF EXERCISES
TO HELP YOU WITH GOAL SETTING,
YOUR VISION, AND YOUR PLAN.

TO ORDER OR LEARN MORE ABOUT
THE BYOB WORKBOOK, VISIT:

BRANDYOUROWN.BUSINESS

VALUES & TRADE SECRETS

"I can't believe you guys share this stuff for free!"

"Thanks for being so willing to share your stuff."

These are a couple of comments we've recently received on our blog at timmilesco.com, where we publish short, thoughtful advice on marketing, communication, leadership, motivation, and productivity.

Why do we share them? Why do we share The First Order of Business?

Because one of our core values is generosity. We freely share what we hope will be better, more useful information to help your business or community organization grow.

We believe that's why we were put on this earth. We believe it's our ministry.

And we believe that good companies and non-profits who like our style and would like to learn more about working with us, will reach out to us to ask about our services. It's why we don't openly solicit business.

We believe we'll grow by helping anyone willing to do the work to grow for free.

And we also believe a few good companies will say, "Wow, if they're willing to share this, I wonder what their secret stuff is?"

Well, yes, we do have diagnostics at each level that we don't share publicly, but it's more about bridging the levels and connecting dots, often dots that other people never see.

THE SECRET TO SUSTAINABLE SUCCESS HAS BEEN INSIDE YOU ALL ALONG... PROBABLY...

You don't get to invent your company's values. You already have them.

They've been deeply entrenched in your company since its history—showing themselves off every day in the way you treat your team and your team's customers. They were likely instilled in you as early as when you were born and nurtured through your experiences and your environments growing up. They were shaped by mentors and also equally by people for whom you had no respect.

Why does this matter? It matters dearly because people no longer simply accept the things you say in your advertising at face value. We're a skeptical society, and rightly so. Too many people have tried to fool us too many times. The world today is not only waiting to hear what you have to say—they're watching to see what you do.

As Gandhi said:

YOUR HABITS DEFINE YOUR VALUES.

Attune your systems, policies, procedures, and customer experience to those values, and be willing to pay the price for the fact that not everyone is going to like you.

Are you willing to be closed on Sundays like Hobby Lobby or Chick-fil-A? Are you willing to avoid producing electric guitars like Martin & Co.?

Or would you prefer not to rock the boat and try and consider everyone your customer? Rather than being something powerful to some smaller section of the population, would you rather try and please everyone?

There's never been a worse time in history for that strategy. It will surely sink you.

WHAT IS A BRAND?

Harley Davidson, Apple, The St. Louis Cardinals... even if, at this point, you're not sure exactly what a brand is, you're pretty sure all three of those are brands, right?

And you're also pretty sure brands are everywhere, aren't you? You're right, of course, but I'm not sure you know just how right you are.

Your grandma.

When you read those words silently to yourself, what mental images come to mind?

The way she looks? The sound of her voice? Maybe a smell of her perfume or her cooking? What about her laugh and the feelings you had of going to grandma's house?

Your grandma is a brand.

A brand is the collection of feelings, sights, smells, tastes, emotions, and sounds that we recall when we think about a person, place, thing, or company.

You don't even need to have met, or done business with that brand, to have an opinion of her, him, or it.

Have you ever met Santa Claus personally? And yet, I'm certain you have very powerful memories and feelings and associations that come with those two simple words.

The same is true for any and all words, though some will have more powerful associations with you than others, and other people will have more powerful associations with other words, thoughts, actions, and ideas.

The question is (and what we hope to help you do throughout the course of this book), how can you grow your powers to harness this magical energy of words, and emotions, and brands?

Peel back this page to the next, and let's begin to build your strong brand foundation, shall we? Wait though, before we get to that, there's one thing we should discuss...

WAIT! ISN'T MY LOGO MY BRAND? WHAT ABOUT MY TAGLINE? AND MY COLOR PALETTE?

Not long ago, my alma mater made headlines for their new logo.

They weren't the good kind of headlines. My university, already under financial duress, commissioned a new logo (that looked remarkably like an old logo) and paid $1,000,000 for the right to use it.

Sigh... I'm going to tell you something that you might not like and most graphic designers you know will hate, but I firmly believe it's for your own good, and I'm happy to have this conversation with anyone who disagrees with me.

Unless your logo is blatantly offensive or obviously illegible, no one... NO ONE... will do business with you because of—or in spite of—your logo... or your tagline... or your color palette. Ever.

Please re-read that paragraph.

Iconography, colors, fonts, tag lines... all these things matter a little, but what really matters are the actions of your team to associate strong, positive feelings of awesome with whatever mark your company uses.

In 20 years, I've never found a designer who can disagree with me, and I love designers. I love great design.

But logo design? Tagline creation? They support only the experiences to which they become anchored... not the other way around.

That agency that hit the $1,000,000 jackpot? I don't blame them... well, I do, a little. They should know better, but it's how they make their living, I suppose, and I certainly don't blame the designer.

But me? I want to talk to the salesperson who convinced the university to pay a million bucks for three letters.

THAT person could sell ice to Eskimos, I reckon...

BUILDING YOUR BRAND DIAMOND

Your brand is a composite of the values you embody that manifest themselves through your observable actions—the list of systems, policies, and procedures that determine how you treat your customers and employees.

I want you to consider your brand a character. Personify it. How does your brand think, act, and see the world? What are the criteria your brand uses to make decisions about pricing, promotion, hiring, firing, and celebrating.

If we're talking character development, let's turn to Hollywood. After all, who does a better job of creating characters that guide us, move us, and make us believe them?

Screenwriting instructor David Freeman introduced me to the concept of a Character Diamond—the values that shape the way a character thinks, acts, and sees the world.

Give a character less than three values, and she's a wooden caricature not worthy of sustained interest.

Give a character more than five values, and she's all over the map. She's unpredictable to the point of distraction and disinterest.

Great characters consistently manifest three to five values that magnetically attract us to them, particularly if we share those values. We see ourselves in them, and it makes us want to follow where they lead.

The "best characters" have one value that's, well, off. Freeman calls this characteristic a "skewed opposite." A skewed opposite refers to an unusually incongruent-but-still-relevant value that gives the character its secret sauce.

Consider Sherlock Holmes—a brilliant, puzzle-solving, antisocial man. Those three values align with one another, giving Holmes a depth we can recognize and find interesting.

But he's also a degenerate drug abuser. He has demons. He has a dark side. This little something that doesn't quite fit the rest of his archetype, and his conflict with it, makes him one of history's great fictional characters.

Your company, your brand, is a character, too. Consumers look at the way your company thinks, acts, and sees the world.

The best way to ensure consistency, and to begin to build a strong brand, is to build your company in your own image, and find that one great thing about you that doesn't quite fit.

For our company, our brand diamond looks something like this:

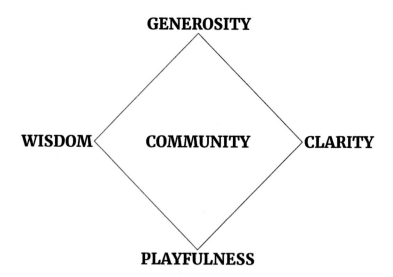

Generosity, Clarity, Wisdom... all three are in the same pew at church, aren't they? These are three things that help make us easy to understand, but it's our fourth, Playfulness, that lends a bit of cayenne pepper to the chocolate.

We don't take ourselves too seriously, and we want to attract companies who feel the same way. And we want to repel companies that do take themselves too seriously.

Notice it's a carefully chosen skewed opposite that often determines the level of attraction or repulsion.

Notice too, there's a fifth word—there at the very core of the diamond. It's at the heart of every thing we do and every decision we make. For us, that's Community, and we have systems, policies, and procedures that reflect that.

What's at the heart of your company? We'll help you uncover that in the next section.

HOW TO UNCOVER YOUR COMPANY'S CORE VALUES

Our team has come up with a series of exercises to help your team uncover your true core values. When you're finished with these exercises, you'll have not only all the raw materials you need to create your brand diamond, but most of the raw materials for exercises in later sections when you create your company's Constitution, Customer Personas, and Copy Right.

Again, gather your team into evenly divided groups and, if possible, mix the departments among the groups. Give them a time limit for each of the following exercises. You may also do this using an online survey software... but if you do so, make it clear *why* you're asking them these questions (I just told you).

EXERCISE #1: THREE WORDS

Ask each group to come up with the three words that best describe your company.

After they're finished have someone write them all down as you go table by table to have one spokesperson from each explain the three words and why they chose them.

Then, once everyone is finished, you're going to ask them to throw away those words. Why? Because while those words may be true, they're utterly predictable and trite. They're the words, consciously or not, your team thinks you want to hear. They're also the words every company chooses. That's where exercise two comes in.

NOTE: It's critical you don't tip your hand to the fact that the words in the first exercise are going to be discarded. They very much matter in so much that we had to have your team get those words out of their collective system before moving on.

EXERCISE #2: FOURTH WORD

Ask your team to come up with one additional word that's just as true as the first three but that no one else on the team will think of. I'm totally serious. Suggest there will be prizes for people who are the sole providers. BUT—and it's a big but—they must also say why this word fits your business. This is a fun exercise. You'll hear laughter. You'll also get teams dropping the aforementioned cat in the aforementioned punchbowl. These are the meaty words you can use to fill out a wicked-good brand diamond and we should see these words or something that demonstrates these words in your UVP.

EXERCISE #3: FAVORITE EMPLOYEE

Tell your teams to go around the table. Tell the rest of your group about your favorite employee (name or don't name names) and why he or she is your favorite team member. Listen for common denominators between your favorite employees. Have one person at each table listen for those common denominators. After 10–15 minutes, have the table spokesperson share those common denominators.

You know what you've just done? Built a composite of your dream employee by building her through a collage of your best and most fervent servant leaders. Well done.

EXERCISE #4: FAVORITE CUSTOMER

This time, you name names as you once again go around the table and tell stories about your favorite customers. Listen for common denominators between your favorite customers. Have one person at each table listen for those common denominators. After three songs (you may need more for this exercise), have the table spokesperson share those common denominators.

You know what you've just done... AGAIN??? Built your ideal customers. You've also outlined your ideal customer's values and defining characteristics using real examples. You've deconstructed your best customer by building her through a collage of your best and most favorite servant leaders, Well done again!

EXERCISE #5: PARTIES

What are the last three things your company celebrated?

We can learn a lot about both your goals and values by the things and people you celebrate. These actions speak volumes to your company.

- Did you celebrate hitting a financial goal?

- Did you celebrate a new business development goal?

- Did you celebrate a customer satisfaction score like CSI or NPS?

- Did you get together to watch the first round of the NCAA Tournament?

- Did you celebrate an employee's birthday? A customer's?

- Did you go to a baseball game together for no particular reason at all?

- Did you simply celebrate the fact that it was Thursday?

Tell me about the last three parties your company threw, and I will tell you about your company.

(If you can't remember the last three parties, or even the last party your company had, then you can probably guess my advice to you).

EXERCISE #5a: COMMUNITY PROJECTS

Same as exercise #4, except brainstorm about ALL the ways your company has given back in your community (or even nationally). To what have you contributed besides your bottom line? These can be individuals in your company or the company as whole.

EXERCISE #6: SIMILARS:

Often, it's hard to read the label when you're inside the bottle... meaning, you're all cursed with the knowledge of your company and your industry and can easily have a blind spot toward things that are really important. It's time to shift your paradigm and get into your right brain for this exercise. It's very simple, yet also sometimes the most challenging.

Ask your teams: "What companies outside our own industry are we most like? What local, national, or international companies are we most like? Why?"

Want to improve your positioning against your competitors? Instead of your competitors, compare yourself to your hero companies—those companies you aspire to be.

Ask your staff to complete two simple exercises. The slightly braver of you will again also ask some customers.

EXERCISE #6a

We're like [aspirational company A], but we _____
_____ .

EXERCISE #6b

We're like [aspirational company A], but they _____
_____.

Pick some national or international companies that inspire you, and do the same exercise substituting them for competitors. How are you like Apple, or Whole Foods, or Disney?

We've been doing this lately with some clients, and the results have been both interesting and helpful.

I bet you find the same will be true for you, too.

Add that this will help transform your policies and procedures.

These discussions are revealing... to hear your team tell you why you're like Disney or Apple or Buc-ee's Travel Mart (or any other local or national business whose experience inspires you) will reveal aspirations, true characteristics, and values that are worth noting and using. (Buc-ee's, by the way, consistently ranks in the top five cleanest bathrooms in America.)

EXERCISE #7: HEROES

If money were no object, who would we have as our spokesperson? Why? Who are your personal and professional heroes? Choose three. With whom—living or dead—would you like to have dinner with to pick their brain? Why? What is it about each person at your table that inspired you to include them over the billions of other people throughout history?

EXERCISE #8: VILLAINS

Who DON'T we want as advocates? Why not? Who is our un-ideal person? What values repel us?

EXERCISE #9: THE DRIVE-YOU-CRAZIES & THE NEVER-EVERS

This one is probably the most fun. Tell your tables: "List out all the stuff our competition and people in our industry do that we'd NEVER do. What drives you crazy? What hurts the credibility of the perception of our profession? Then list what you'd do differently."

While you should not trash your competition in your marketing or in your unique value proposition, you will want to have a list of these things, and in your own marketing you'll focus on what you do differently. This is another way of doing a more global version of the positioning wedge exercise we'll talk about in the Strategic Planning section of this book.

ONE MORE EXERCISE... IT'S WEIRD: WRITE A LETTER.

Have each member of your team write a letter that will help you flesh out the second why of your new, improved value statement. These letters will help you understand, in simple non-marketing language, your team's true motivations, passions, and intrinsic beliefs.

Ask your team: "Write a letter to someone, dead or alive, for whom you have the utmost respect. Tell them about what you do, how you help people, and tell them why you get out of bed each morning to go do what you do."

You might consider giving this last assignment as homework. Give each of them a day or a week to work on the letter. And recognize this letter is hard work! Reward each team member who completes it (not all will) with a gift card or other nice treat.

These exercises will give you more valuable insight and content for your marketing than any high-paid ad firm could invent for you. What you're getting here is relevant, credible intel on how and why you are in the business that you're in.

ASK YOUR CUSTOMERS A SIMPLE QUESTION

Sometimes it's hard to see yourself for who you really are. If you feel that might be the case, ask your customers—either while serving them or using your email list—one simple question:

"What are the first words that come to mind when you think about us? Why those words?"

Collect these answers. Study them. See if any particular value rises to the top.

HAVE YOU UNCOVERED THE RIGHT VALUES?

Let's reiterate: There's nothing inherently wrong with the first three words the members of your team choose in the first core value exercise. I assure you those words are not only accurate and inspiring, but they're also ubiquitous! Everyone uses them. Remember, these values establish the very foundation upon which you'll grow this company throughout this generation and beyond. Let's make sure their as unique as the DNA that makes up you and your company.

Let me give you an example: Patrick Morin owns and operates Roof Life of Oregon in Portland. He's been not only a client for a decade but also a good friend, mentor, and brother to me.

And before we had an in-depth discussion of values, he had done something really cool.

 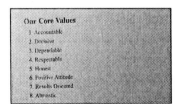

On his own, Patrick had his company's core values printed on the back of every team member's business cards. Isn't that brilliant? What a wonderful way to communicate what the company stands for!

I thought, however, it could be improved. I can't think of a company who *doesn't* value those eight principles (with the possible exception of the eighth), can you? So, we worked with Patrick and his team to uncover fourth words... words that are still strong reflections of how the company thinks, acts, and sees the world, but are far more interesting, evocative and unique to Roof Life of Oregon.

Their new business cards are on the top of the next page. They uncovered all the new value words.

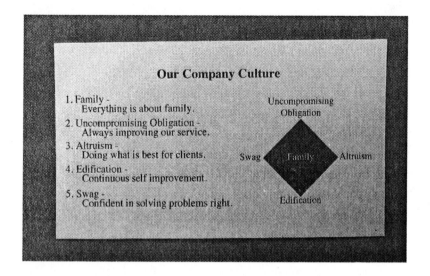

CRAFTING YOUR COMPANY'S PURPOSE

What is a Unique Value Proposition (UVP)? I'm glad you asked. Having recently spent more hours than I care to count online researching them, I feel I'm probably as qualified as anyone to answer this question for you.

Before I give you my answer, I will tell you that my research showed two things:

1. Ask 50 different experts about a UVP, and you'll get 50 different answers. Mine's no different or better, I suppose, so you should take that with a grain of salt... except to say that mine is well-researched and deeply rooted in common sense.

2. And this may surprise you, but do you know what the difference is between the following?

- a unique value proposition

- a unique selling proposition

- a statement of values

- a statement of principles

- a credo

- a mission statement

Nothing. Really. Go spend countless hours researching them and see for yourself.

And there's nothing so much problematic about the first five, but the sixth causes lots of good, smart people to roll their eyes.

We've grown to hate mission statements... at least that's what modern conventional wisdom seems to indicate.

But I disagree slightly. I want to amend that to say we don't hate mission statements, but rather we hate *bad* mission statements.

We hate cliché-filled, rainbow-unicorny mission statements. We hate mission statements for software companies that could be swapped with mission statements for cancer centers because they're both filled with such ambiguous language that they mean nothing that matters to anyone.

There's a formula, too, to building one of these:

Who? What? How?

Who's our customer?

What do we do?

How do we do it?

Really, go Google your favorite company, or your competitor, and find their mission statement on their website. I promise you if you do this with more than ten companies, you can create your own Mission Statement MadLibs because they're all virtually following that same template.

You know why? It's one of two reasons:

1. They hired a marketing firm to invent a mission statement for them.

A mission statement or unique value proposition can't be invented. It already exists based upon the values and actions of the company and how it treats its employees and customers.

2. The executive team (possibly with help from the marketing department) looked up mission statements on the Internet and picked one they liked and then tried to edit it to fit who they thought they wanted to be in the eyes of customers.

You know what's missing?

The formula: Who? Who? How? Why? Why?

Who are we?

Who's our customer?

How do we serve them?

Why is serving them important to us?

Why should it matter to the customer?

If you want to turn your bland, average mission statement into a company purpose that's meaningful to both customers and employees, chances are two things are missing from your current mission statement:

1.	The real "why"—that passion behind what makes the employees of a company get out of bed to do what they do.

2.	The employees didn't create it. Mission statements, UVPs, USPs have to be *owned* by a company's employees... but too often, they have it told to them like other company policies or procedures.

To matter, a statement like this has to be uncovered by your entire team.

The good news? You've already done it!

We started this section by talking about your goals—your mission—and we then concluded this chapter by uncovering your values.

You now have everything you need to determine your company's purpose.

MISSION + VALUES = PURPOSE

Your mission is where you're going, and your values are the tools you'll use to help you get there. Ask your team to write—in no more than 50 words—a statement of purpose for your company using only the tools of your clear vision and your brand diamond.

Tell us where you're going. Tell us how you'll help people along the way. Tell us why they need you. Tell us why it matters so much to you.

Congratulations! Your company has a clear purpose that should be placed prominently throughout your company. You and your team have cemented a clear, meaningful purpose for your company. You've developed goals. You've identified your company's core values.

Finally, by uncovering your true core values, you've assembled the fundamental tools you'll use to identify, develop, and refine the systems, policies, and procedures you'll use. You've also established the elements of your customer experience and messaging strategies.

TIM MILES & COMPANY'S PURPOSE

Tim Miles & Company is a small* business that helps other small businesses communicate more powerfully by being true to and proud of who they are and how they serve.

With so much information—and misinformation—out there about marketing and management consulting, we want our clients to tell others we're the least full of crap people they've ever heard on the subjects by being clear, generous, and well-researched. We'll help them using our First Order of Business Methodology.

We believe small businesses and community organizations are—and will continue to be—the foundation of this and other countries, and they deserve the best information they can find on marketing, management, and motivation in this age of rapid distraction so they can efficiently and effectively serve their communities—both with their services and through their modeling of leadership for others.

If you've ever owned or worked in one for very long, you know it's anything but small. It's usually your whole world. It keeps you up nights. It fills you with the highest of highs and lowest of lows. We understand completely.

ISN'T THIS AN AWFUL LOT OF WORK??

"He erected the court all around the tabernacle and the altar, and hung up the veil for the gateway of the court. Thus Moses finished the work." - Exodus 40:33 (NASB)

I was reading my Bible last week (okay, technically, I was reading my Bible app) when I found myself stuck on this particular passage. Specifically, I kept focusing on one sentence:

"Moses finished the work."

In this chapter, Moses is setting up the tabernacle just as God had instructed him. Moses could've said, "Hey, God! You created the entire universe. Why do you need me? Just snap your fingers and set up your own tabernacle!"

But Moses didn't do that. Moses finished the work.

When we do speaking engagements or workshops we usually begin by saying, "If you're here to learn about a magic marketing pill or secret advertising recipe that will make your business grow overnight, you've come to the wrong place. We are the diet and exercise of advertising."

In other words, we can equip you with the tools, knowledge, and resources, but you have to do the work. Nobody is going to do it for you. After all, if Moses couldn't get a Get-Out-Of-Work-Free Card, what makes you think you deserve one?

Will it take longer? Yes. Will it be more difficult? Yes.

Nobody said it would be easy.

Do the work.

The magic pill doesn't exist. Sure, there are gimmicks and sales tricks that may work in the short term. But just like the latest diet fad, the more you do it, the less effective it becomes. So you move on to the next gimmick, hoping it will succeed. (Spoiler alert: It won't).

Stop searching for a sack of magic business beans.

Stop making excuses.

Stop feeling sorry for yourself.

Stop expecting someone else to do it for you.

Do what Moses did. Put on your big boy pants and finish the work.

Lead by example and focus your team. Equip them with not only the tools they need but the confidence to use them and the belief in you as their leader on this mission.

They're looking to you. Are you ready?

IN THE WORKBOOK VERSION OF
BRAND YOUR OWN BUSINESS,
WE PROVIDE 20 PAGES OF
EXERCISES TO HELP YOU AND YOUR
TEAM UNCOVER YOUR VALUES
AND REFINE YOUR PURPOSE.

TO ORDER OR LEARN MORE ABOUT
THE BYOB WORKBOOK, VISIT:

BRANDYOUROWN.BUSINESS

NOW, TAKE A LITTLE BREAK.
YOU'VE WORKED REALLY HARD ON
WHAT HAD TO BE DONE.

BECAUSE, TO START THE NEXT
SECTION, I HAVE SOME KIND OF
BAD NEWS...

> "One of the greatest ways to avoid trouble is to keep it simple. When you make it vastly complicated—and only a few high priests in each department can pretend to understand it—what you're going to find all too often is that those high priests don't really understand it at all.... The system often goes out of control.

CHARLIE MUNGER

May 2008

SECTION TWO

STRATEGIC PLANNING

STRATEGIC PLANNING

YOUR VALUES MEAN NOTHING...

Seriously?? THAT'S how you're coming back after all my hard work? Sorta. Let me finish that sentence:

"Your values mean nothing unless you tie them to systems, policies, and procedures—observable actions—that benefit your team and/or your customers."

Once you're secure in your values and prioritized goals, you have to look at how you're going to accomplish your goals, wearing those values. You also need to know, even armed with those values, what limiting factors stand in (or sit, or occasionally lean into) your way?

You need a strategic marketing plan to create these systems, policies, and procedures—all observable behaviors to either your team or your customers—that nullify those limiting factors. We have ten:

1. Business Model

2. Walking the Talk

3. Your Market Potential & Share

4. Your Competition

5. Your Marketing Budgets

6. Your Customers

7. Your Blind Spots

8. Your Warranties, Assurances, and Guarantees

9. Your Causes

10. Your Team

If your goals are realistic, and your values are true, the strength of your strategic plan will ultimately determine the strength of your brand.

Do you have a clear path to where you want to go? Have you clearly identified the obstacles in your way? Without making time to do so, you can—now more than ever—waste horrific amounts of money.

And that would kind of stink, wouldn't it?

Here's the great news: This section is full of actionable techniques and tactics to elevate your business and strengthen your position in your market. It will make you think about where your brand belongs in the marketplace and how to make it more relevant and credible. When you've completed this section and its exercises, you're going to be powerfully confident in how best to use your values to position yourself against your competitors and delight your customers and employees.

BUSINESS MODEL

Even if your ultimate 20-year vision is to change the world, how are you going to fund your world-changing?

Clearly knowing your path to *revenue*—and having that path make economic sense—is as simple a definition of business model as I can muster. As a responsible business owner, I also believe your business model must include a path to *profitability*.

Others, including many of today's dot-com entrepreneurs, see it a little bit differently than I do.

The New Math... not the Same as the Old Math...

When I read internet audio hosting site SoundCloud received another $70mm in debt funding in March of 2017 and saw it juxtaposed to this revenue-vs-net-loss chart on the next page from Music Business Worldwide, I wondered if Silicon Valley hadn't either lost its collective mind or hoped they'd live long enough to survive their Madoff-like Ponzi parade to retreat to their solar-powered palapas in non-extradition countries.

The more they earn, the more they lose? Am I reading that right? Are you reading that right?

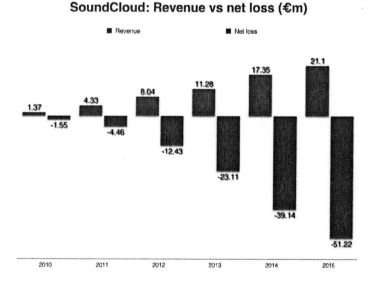

SoundCloud: Revenue vs net loss (€m)

What gives?

In his 2016 book, *Disrupted: My Misadventures in the Start-Up Bubble,* respected journalist Dan Lyons recounts his eye-opening entrance as a 50-year-old into the world of

HubSpot, an inbound-marketing company. In a chapter entitled "The New Work," Lyons quotes a friend—an investment banker—who's watched the rise and rise and rise and rise and plummet and ridiculous resurrection of this brave new world closely:

> *"It's all about the business model. The market pays you to have a company that scales quickly. It's all about getting big fast. Don't be profitable, just get big."*

Lyons follows up:

> *That's what HubSpot is doing. Its technology isn't very impressive, but look at that revenue growth! That's why venture capitalists have sunk so much money into HubSpot, and why they believe HubSpot will have a successful IPO. That's also why HubSpot hires so many young people. That's what investors want to see: a bunch of young people, having a blast, talking about changing the world. It sells.*

If this business model intrigues you... if this sounds like a brass-plated silicon ring for which you'd like to reach, stop reading. This ain't the book for you, Unicorn Pants.

Peter Drucker and Preventive Care

In 1994, the late management genius Peter Drucker published an article in *Harvard Business Review* about what he called **The Theory of the Business.**

While not specifically using the words "business model," Drucker comprehensively analyzed which mechanics, wheels, and pulleys it took to successfully grow and sustain a business.

One tool he recommends using to ensure your business model—your path to revenue—remains successful is "Preventive Care."

Drucker suggests a method of abandonment:

> *Every three years, an organization should challenge every product, every service, every policy, every distribution channel with the question, If we were not in it already, would we be going into it now? By questioning accepted policies and routines, the organization forces itself to think about its theory. It forces itself to test assumptions. It forces itself to ask: Why didn't this work, even though it looked so promising when we went into it five years ago? Is it because we made a mistake? Is it because we did the wrong things? Or is it because the right things didn't work?*

By doing this, Drucker says, your business will remain agile and prepared to adapt as markets shift.

This echoes an analysis done by the authors of the Foreword to this book.

Be Like Amazon

In May of 2017, on the 20th anniversary of its initial public offering, Amazon became as large as TWO Wal-Marts. Did you ever think that possible? Jeff Bezos did, and so did Jeffrey and Bryan Eisenberg. The Eisenbergs, along with

Roy H. Williams, authored *Be Like Amazon: Even A Lemonade Stand Can Do It* in early 2017.

In their work, they examined what they considered to be the four pillars of Amazon's success. These fou pillars fold nicely into Drucker's Theory of the Business. The Eisenbergs and Williams write:

> *In 1994, Jeff Bezos committed Amazon.com to become "earth's most customer-centric company." Amazon's long-term focus is on staying ahead of their customers, not competitors. It is all based on four simple pillars that every company can leverage.*
>
> *The Four Pillars of Amazon's Success:*
>
> - *Customer Centricity*
> - *Continuous Optimization*
> - *Culture of Innovation*
> - *Corporate Agility*
>
> *These are the essence of the Amazon brand. Look closely and you'll see that the four pillars of Amazon's success speed each other up. They create a virtuous flywheel that spins at ever-greater speeds.*

You may think Amazon's no different than SoundCloud or Hubspot, that its mere goal is to be big, not profitable. You, like many, might believe Amazon may be big, but it's never turned a profit. Not so, you learn in *Be Like Amazon:*

That's a popular myth, but it's not true. Amazon became profitable in the 4th quarter of 2001 when they reported a net income of $5 million. In 2003, net revenue grew to $5.26 billion, and they had a $35 million net profit. In 2015 they became the fastest company to ever reach $100 billion in annual sales, and they also happened to generate $8 billion in free cash flow after all the bills were paid and all the investments were made. Fifty percent of all e-commerce went through Amazon that year, and the percentage is going up.

Here's a graphic the authors created to illustrate how Amazon perpetually builds up intertia. Fascinating, isn't it? It's also profitable.

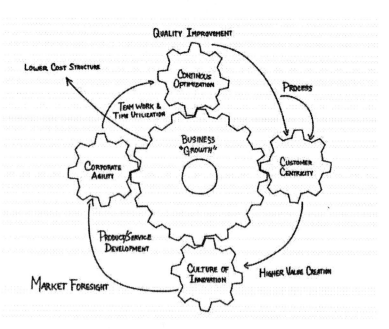

I highly recommend this book. It's a quick read, and in a space filled with haughty technofluff, the Eisenbergs and

Williams distill the practical applications of technological change into a simple, thoughtful, delightful story. The writing is crisp. The tips are relevant. The haughty technofluff is notably—and pleasantly—absent.

Simplify. Simplify. Simplify.

> *The question isn't, "What do I want to get done in the next thirty days?" but, "Who do I want to become in this next season of my life?"* –Bill Hybels

Hybels' delightful book, *Simplify*, reminds us to see the forest for the trees, but just as we spent the first section of this book defining what that forest means to us, we must have a plan to grow it. Knowing what you want to become is essential, yes—but how will you acquire the provisions for your journey?

That's where business model comes in:

1. How will you generate revenue in a way that makes economic sense?

2. What consumer itch are you scratching? How will you help people in a way that makes them give you money?

3. What mechanics do you have in place to review your model and make sure it's malleable with time, technology, and the tools at your disposal?

Know your business model. Understand your path to revenue and profit. Make sure your team knows not only who you want to become and where you're going but also how you're going to get there.

IT'S TIME TO FIND OUT IF YOU WALK THE TALK

So, not unlike a parent of a child or puppy, you're incredibly proud of the core values you uncovered in section one.

As well you should be! You went through some serious soul-searching, and not just you, but your entire team really dug deep to find the authentic way your company thinks, acts, and sees the world.

But for now, they're just really cool... words. And if your actions don't match up with those words, then those words actually hurt your business; they don't help.

You literally need to list out each way a system, policy, and procedure reflects a core value and how those observable actions benefit your team or your customers or both.

I'm completely serious.

To amplify your signal above the white noise of clever clamoring with pretty ignorance, you need weight behind your words.

We want you to survey your team, and we want you to reward them for their efforts. One client of ours put the name attached to every completed survey into a hat and drew out three and gave each $150. (This won't be the last time you reward employees for identifying ways you walk the talk).

Feeble brands are weak for one of two reasons:

1. They're not connected to anything we care about. They don't have a killer set of core values.

2. They don't walk the talk. They picked a great set of words, but those words ring hollow to both employees and customers.

The first reason makes you irrelevant. The second makes you a liar. Neither gives you a chance.

How Does the Survey Work?

You're literally going to list out the words in your brand diamond and add a few of the other more interesting, unique values words that came out of the survey (you might need them), and you're going to ask your team for each word:

WHAT SYSTEMS, POLICIES, PROCEDURES—OR OTHER OBSERVABLE ACTIONS BY CUSTOMERS AND EMPLOYEES—DEMONSTRATE/MANIFEST [VALUE A]? ALSO, HOW DO YOU THINK EACH ONE BENEFITS THE CUSTOMER OR EMPLOYEE?

You're going to repeat this question with each of the value words in your diamond and the additional words you choose.

We cannot over-stress how valuable these survey results will be to you. They will separate you as wheat from your competitors' chaff. They will prove to employees and customers alike that you're relevant, that you're credible, and that you're a company that can be known, liked, and trusted.

But what if people don't like my values or our systems, policies, and procedures?

Some will not, and that's okay. In the Age of Rapid Distraction, when we're drowning in noise and exhausted by options, we desperately try to connect with people and companies who share—truly share—our values.

As Patricia Cabot said, "You're not a $100 bill. Not everybody's going to like you."

And that's okay... because when you think about the size of your market and your potential in it, you quickly realize there should be more than enough potential customers who share your values to leave you without such worries.

Don't worry about trying to be, say, Chick-fil-A... or The Grateful Dead... be you... you are more than good enough!

YOUR MARKET POTENTIAL & SHARE

A Shockingly Accurate Way to Calculate Market Potential and Your Share of It

In terms of share of market, know that it's much easier to gain share when you're small. While there are exceptions to every rule, they do not disprove them, and the rule is that a market giant in a typical town with a typical number of competitors will have no higher than a 30% market share. There are simply too many other customers who have too many reasons to do business with your competitors (geography, friends and family relationships, lower prices for customers who don't value your quality of service, etc.). Experience has also taught us that once you hit somewhere between 30-33%, it becomes very difficult to grow unless you're willing to add services or grow geographically by adding locations.

So, what's yours?

We're guessing you don't know how much your competitors are doing each year, but I bet you're wiser than you think.

Want to calculate both your market potential (the total amount being spent in your category in your market) and your share of that potential?

We know it's shockingly accurate because we've been having clients do it this way for close to ten years, and we've been comparing their results to a proprietary method we use to calculate market potential. They're always within shouting distance of one another, and once we share the steps with you, it won't surprise you why that's the case.

WARNING: We *know* this isn't exact, but why not try it?

1. Gather everyone in your company who's been working for you—or originally worked for one of your competitors and now works for you—for at least a year. You want people with knowledge of your market, your industry, and your competitors. You should expose newer employees to the process, but their answers will likely hurt your sample.

2. Ask each person to write down—separately and without comparing answers—every competitor you have. Tell them to really think about it. Try and think of all the small, even one-person, shops that compete with you. List them all out.

3. Now, next to each competitor, have them guess what each of your competitor's annual revenues are—if that's your metric.

4. Collect everyone's sheets of paper and bust out your spreadsheet app. For each competitor, take the average of everyone's guesses to come up with estimated revenue per competitor.

5. Add up the average estimated revenues of each competitor and add your own revenue. This will give you an eerily accurate estimate of the total dollars spent in your market in your business category.

6. Divide your revenue by the answer to #5 above (total dollars spent in your market in your business

category), and you've got your estimated market share. I'd be surprised if your answer turns out to be much different than what you'd get using our double-triple-secret way of calculating market potential. It rarely is.

YOUR COMPETITION

Positioning Wedges

"Every Goliath Has a Stone" read a church sign in middle Tennessee.

Think about your two or three biggest competitors. List them out on paper. Stuff gets more real when you put it down on paper.

Now, answer this question for each competitor:

IN WHAT WAY, OR WAYS, DOES (COMPETITOR) FALL SHORT/ UNDERWHELM IN SERVING ITS CUSTOMERS?

Then, follow up with:

WHAT DO WE DO DIFFERENTLY?

HOW DO WE OVERCOME THESE SHORTCOMINGS?

After you've answered these questions, ask each of your employees the same questions (the slightly more daring of you will also ask your regular customers). Do not let them collaborate. You want as many different answers as possible.

Most powerful advertising comes from systems, policies, and procedures that differentiate you from your competitors in your customers' eyes.

Sure, ad writers can dazzle people with fluff, even moving, or hilarious, or brilliant fluff. But that's getting harder by the day, because there are thousands of brilliant pieces of fluff out there these days. Plus, brilliant fluff fades more quickly than ever.

To win, your marketing person needs meaty bits and stories showing how those meaty bits benefited real customers.

The answers to these questions will provide your company, and your marketing department, with a feast full of awesome.

YOUR MARKETING BUDGETS

I get asked "How do I determine how much I should spend on marketing and advertising?" as much as any question, I suppose, and I admire it for two reasons:

1. It shows strategic thought about marketing and advertising as a necessary, calculated expense.

2. When budgeting long-term for marketing, you can save yourself a lot of money by buying in bulk or buying in advance. In this way, media channels are no more or less a commodity than forms, coffee, or paper towels.

With new clients, this is typically where I ask the question: "Well, what's the difference between marketing and advertising?" I'm often met with blank stares.

You see, we focus so hard on acquiring new customers (often at great expense) that we forget how important it is to remember those who've already trusted us with their business.

Therefore, I suggest breaking up your total marketing budget into two parts: New Customer Acquisition and Customer Retention & Increase. This might be scary to you at first because it goes against everything you've ever done. Start small—budget 20% to customer retention, then plan on increasing it until it's a full third of your total marketing budget.

For the purposes of calculation below, I'm referring to your total marketing budget—new customer acquisition plus customer retention.

Typically, we see most businesses calculate their marketing budgets as a percentage (typically 3-10%) of sales, and that's a great baseline to establish an annual number; however, several factors can affect this baseline number.

(Before getting into these factors, note that your company should plan to spend that three to ten percent based on next year's projected sales).

LONGEVITY – A company that has a foothold in the market has built up generational equity to make themselves a household name. For this reason alone, a 60-year-old company may spend closer to 3% than 10% since their goal may be to hang on to their current market share or use their entrenched network of repeat and referral business to help them increase their market share.

COMPETITIVE ENVIRONMENT

There are three factors here:

1. How good are your competitors?

2. How well-known are your competitors?

3. What are their perceived reputations in the market?

We suspect you can estimate answers to each of these questions given your unique knowledge of your industry and your market.

PHYSICAL PLANT VISIBILITY

How are your locations? Do people drive past you every day? While there are not necessarily any emotional anchors associated with seeing you every day, it doesn't hurt for unaided recall to have a highly visible location. Sometimes, the cheapest advertising is expensive rent. Conversely, if your location limits the amount of drive-by traffic everyday, you're going to have to factor in a higher percentage of sales to your budget.

PHYSICAL PLANT RENT

If you have low rent or own your building, you have a tremendous opportunity to infuse your marketing budget with that capital. Don't fret about this. Remember, we are making over your marketing so it's an asset, not a liability.

GOOGLE / SEO

Organically speaking, how well does Google know you and respect you by ranking you at the top of its search engine ranking positions (SERPs) for your name and your services (keyword searches)?

REPUTATION

Organically speaking, how highly does your market think of you? How are your online reviews in places like Google, Yelp!, Facebook, and Angry's, err, Angie's List? Have you registered with the proper online directories?

MARKUP/MARGIN

Let's be frank… if you make more money on your goods and services because you mark them up higher than average, you can and should spend a larger percentage of your sales on marketing and advertising. Don't look at this as a negative. Remember, this book and your training in the good principles of the first four tiers of The First Order of Business will help you make this larger spend a great investment.

MARKET

$60,000 in Nashville, Tennessee, is very different from $60,000 in Hohenwald, Tennessee. You may not like the tax you pay for living in a large market, but you have more potential customers in exchange for that tax. You also have more noise to be heard above. You also have more options for takeout... which is always a good thing.

If this were easy, everyone would be doing it well.

The Math of Good Customers

Seven Questions. Ready? Begin.

1. What's the value of a customer over the course of her lifetime?

We want you to picture a regular customer, and we want you to think about how much that customer's average ticket is and how often they buy from you. Multiply the average ticket by number of visits between now and when she no longer needs what you sell.

But you're not done. Your customer-for-life has friends, doesn't she? If you're as good as she says you are, her friends are going to want to do business with you, too, aren't they? Let's say she brings you just two percent of the people with whom she's close... a number which I happen to know is about three people.

Let's multiply her personal lifetime value by 4. Write that number down and set it aside.

2. How much does it cost to acquire a new customer?

This is also pretty easy to calculate for most companies. Let's take last year's total marketing budget and divide it by the number of new customers you acquired last year. That gives us our cost of customer acquisition.

3. How much does each lead cost?

Just like customer acquisition, take last year's total marketing budget and divide it by the number of leads you earned last year. That gives you your cost per lead.

4. What's your conversion/closing rate?

Divide your number of new customers by your leads. That's how many customers you converted/closed from the number of leads you earned.

5. How much do you want to grow?

Provided it's not obviously impossible, this number's entirely up to you and your market potential. If you did the previous exercise, you have your shockingly accurate estimate of market potential.

6. Last year, what percentage of your advertising budget do you feel you wasted?

My colleagues and I have asked this question of several thousand family business, and we've found the wastage across all business categories ranges between 50-90%. It may make you feel queasy looking at all those wasted dollars, but at least the facts are on the table.

7. What kind of customers do you want to retain?

Describe what they're like. Do they have common characteristics? The answer to that question is a hearty "yes," because you had your team share their favorite customer stories during your goal-setting and value-uncovering retreat. What are their common characteristics?

ANYONE WHO TRIES BEING ALL THINGS TO ALL PEOPLE WILL SOON FIND THEMSELVES BEING NOTHING TO NO ONE.

Remember what Patricia Cabot said. You're going to be far more successful and sustainable by preaching to the choir of customers that resonate with your values and the systems, policies, and procedures that manifest themselves from those values.

What do these numbers tell you?

They usually tell us it's much more profitable (and fun) to delight your current customers than acquire new ones.

We're not saying it's not worth doing some of both. We're simply saying you might consider moving some of your advertising budget into your customer retention budget.

You do have one of those, don't you?

What goes into your customer retention budget?

Thoughtful, simple, classy messaging that reflects your values and those of your customers. Hand-written, hand-addressed birthday or anniversary cards. Gift cards. Brainstorm with your team and ask for their ideas on ways to reward your best customers. Additionally, the customer retention budget includes your allotment for Shareworthy Customer Service, which we'll discuss at length in the next section.

One More Budget: The Knucklehead Budget

Do you have a knucklehead budget? It's not financial; it's emotional, but it's no less important than any other budget in your business or household.

Knuckleheads wreck stuff, especially stuff that starts out good. Like this bit of good stuff my friend Professor Joey shared with us. In a *CBS Moneywatch* story, Michael Hess (MH) writes about his son being stranded at O'Hare airport with no money to buy a meal. Hess unsuccessfully tried to share his credit card over the phone with three airport restaurants before speaking with someone on staff at Wolfgang Puck Express (WPE):

> *MH: "Is there any way you can take my card and charge his meal? I'll send a picture of the card, whatever you need to feel comfortable."*

WPE: "Unfortunately, we have no way of taking a credit card over the phone..."

MH (assuming that was the end of the sentence): "But, there must be some..."

WPE: "..so just send your boy in here and we'll make sure he gets a good meal. My store manager and operations manager are both here, and we don't want him to be sitting around hungry. You don't have to worry about paying for it."

MH (lump in throat): "Wha... you... no, please, I really insist you find a way for me to pay for this."

WPE: "Just do something nice for someone else."

This happened, folks. Word for word, just like that.

Great, right! But we both know what's going to happen. Within hours (if not minutes) of the "kindness of strangers" story spreading across the Internet, some knucklehead's going to try to take advantage of their kindness and scam free pizza. We wouldn't put it past someone to send their kid into the restaurant while they lurk around the corner.

Puck's is going to need a knucklehead budget. Puck's needs to emotionally prepare for the fact that, yes, some people suck, but doing the right thing in spite of the sucky people is sooooooooo worth it.

Until we can bring a lawsuit against them (think US v. People Who Ruin Everything), we have two choices:

1. Stop doing nice things because it's just not worth the hassle.

2. Acknowledge there are jerks everywhere and make an emotional withdrawal from our knucklehead budget. Just keep doing good deeds even if some Baddy Badderson occasionally takes advantage.

Ignore the loud bleating of the troll. Stay generous. Do good deeds. Be awesome.

YOUR CUSTOMERS

There Are Really Only Two Types of Customers – Which Will You Target?

This chapter's provided by Roy H. Williams with his permission.

Every person has a transactional mode and a relational mode of shopping. And "the right thing to say" can be determined only when you know which mode the shopper is in:

The defining characteristics of Transactional Shoppers are as follows:

1. Transactional shoppers are focused only on today's transaction and give little thought to the possibility of future purchases.

2. Their only fear is of paying more than they had to pay. Transactional shoppers are looking for price and value.

3. They enjoy the process of comparing and negotiating and will likely shop at several stores before making their decision to purchase.

4. Transactional shoppers do their own research so they won't need the help of an expert. *Consumer Reports* are published primarily for the transactional shopper.

5. Because they enjoy the process, transactional shoppers don't consider their time spent shopping to be part of the purchase price.

6. Anxious to share the "good deal" they've found, transactional shoppers are excellent sources of word-of-mouth advertising.

Now, Relational Shoppers, on the other hand...

1. Relational shoppers consider today's transaction to be one in a long series of many future purchases. They are looking less for a product than for a store in which to buy it.

2. Their only fear is of making a poor choice. Relational shoppers will purchase as soon as they have confidence. Will your store and your staff give them this confidence they seek?

3. They don't enjoy the process of shopping and negotiating.

4. Relational shoppers are looking principally for an expert they can trust.

5. They consider their time to be part of the purchase price.

6. Confident that they have found "the right place to buy," relational shoppers are very likely to become repeat customers.

As was stated earlier, every person has a transactional mode and a relational mode of shopping, so don't be surprised when you see yourself in both descriptions. You, like all other shoppers, are extremely transactional in certain product and service categories and wholly relational in others. At any given time and in any given category, about one half of all shoppers will be in transactional mode and the other half will be in relational mode. I can't fully prove this assertion, but I'm sure that someday it will be proven.

Due to the fact that shoppers in transactional mode will shop all over town and love to negotiate, merchants often wrongfully conclude that most shoppers stay in transactional mode. But in truth, more purchases are quietly made by customers in relational mode.

Here's a simple illustration: Two transactional shoppers go to 5 stores each before making their decisions to purchase. At each of these 5 stores, they ask a lot of questions, then leave. But each transactional shopper will return to only one store to make a purchase. This means that a total of 12 store visits will be made by the transactional duo, and 8 different salespeople will be frustrated by them. Meanwhile, 3 relational customers visit their favorite stores, make their purchases and return home, accounting for a total of 3 store visits, 3 purchases, and zero frustrated salespeople. The 2 transactional shoppers account for 80% of all store visits, but only 40% of sales. Conversely, the 3 relational shoppers account for just 20% of total store traffic, but contribute a whopping 60% of the sales volume.

Bottom line: There is no "perfect ad." The right thing to say to a relational shopper is the wrong thing to say to a transactional one. The secret to attracting and keeping happy customers is to communicate the truth about who and what you really are. Remember, you're not a $100 bill. Not everyone is going to like you.

Is your company transactional or relational? Changing your ads so that they speak to a different shopper is easy. But changing the essence of your customer's experience (selection, prices, sales staff) is not.

(Roy H. Williams is Tim's friend, business partner, and Marketing Yoda. Learn more about Roy at www.RHW.com)

An Example of Relational vs. Transactional Strategies in the World of BBQ Catering

Want a real life example of relational versus transaction business models? One company-our client-is vastly more successful than the other. Let's see if you can guess which is which:

Barbecue restaurant #1 in town caters for $7.50 a plate.

That includes two meats, three sides, and a bill.

You don't get plates or napkins or serving spoons.

Oh, and you're serving 3,000, or you're a regular customer and ask for a discount?

Sure thing. For you, it's only $7.50 a plate.

Barbecue restaurant #2 in my town caters for $9.95 a plate.

That includes 2 meats, three sides, utensils, napkins, plates, serving spoons, and moist towelettes.

The business owner has flexibility and headroom (or margin) to make anyone he so chooses feel like they're getting a deal.

Whether it's a large order or a regular customer, business #2 builds in flexibility to ensure he can play favorites and leverage the shareworthy facet of privilege.

We're not saying one strategy's better than the other, but one's probably a lot more fun.

(Okay, we are actually saying one strategy is better than the other...)

YOUR BLIND SPOTS

Mac and Denise McIntosh are the kind of people you want as friends and clients. They're the very best kind of crazy.

In a recent call with their senior staff, Mac shared a great, but really hard question that he had asked his team. We all need to ask our employees this question today.

PLEASE TELL ME: WHAT ARE TWO THINGS YOU DON'T THINK I WANT TO HEAR ABOUT OUR COMPANY?

And here's a second part to that question:

How would you go about improving them?

And that's not the end of this, it's just the beginning (told you it was really hard). It's going to lead to a series of conversations. But these conversations will be a springboard for you all to work together to improve your company.

Another Way of Asking...

Whenever we're hired by a new client, it's non-negotiable that at least two members of our team fly, drive, bike, or trike to their market for two days to get to know them, their company, their city, their competitors, and their culture.

But before we do, we send both a series of prep questions for the owners and an anonymous survey to their employees where they are encouraged to speak frankly for the good of the business and to identify blind spots. The latest question added to our anonymous employee survey?

"If you owned the company, what would you do differently and why?"

Isn't that a billion-dollar question? It's simple, yet it's so much better than the ever-present "if you had a magic wand" question because it raises the (hypothetical) stakes for the employee anonymously answering the question. It also communicates that this new marketing company (us) reinforces—through our First Order of Business framework—that it's not optional to listen to employees, it's mandatory.

Our new super survey question not only has the potential to reveal numerous blind spots to the owners, but it also announces (or reinforces) a Culture of Ownership among the employees. Be prepared to possibly have your feelings hurt... but get over it... and give thanks you have employees who care enough to want to help you grow your company. Be prepared to share the results. Be prepared to take action.

Bottlenecks

Another eye-opening question:

WHAT POINT IN THE CUSTOMER PROCESS, FROM BEGINNING TO END, CLOGS US UP THE MOST? WHY? HOW CAN IT BE FIXED?

Then fix. Reward the suggestions that yield results.

YOUR WARRANTIES, ASSURANCES, AND GUARANTEES

No Wimpy Warranties!

The only thing worse than not having a guarantee? Having a pantywaist guarantee.

I was ordering new socks—yes, I am the most boring person you know—and I came across Darn Tough Socks. I'm a sucker for great, American-made stuff, and that led me to their site, where I found this guarantee:

> *OUR LIFETIME GUARANTEE: Unconditional lifetime guarantee—simply and without strings or conditions—if our socks are not the most comfortable, durable and best fitting socks you have ever owned, return them for another pair, or your money back. No strings. No conditions. For life. When you are really serious about something you make it yourself.*

> *RETURNING SOCKS: If you were able to wear out a pair of Darn Tough socks, we'll replace them. At any time. Just package the socks up, fill out the form, and send to the appropriate address—we will send you a brand new pair!*

> *Don't like these socks ten years later? Return them. Wear out a pair of these socks in thirty years? Exchange them.*

Most companies, sadly, stop at "if you don't like them, return them within 14 days of purchase, and we'll refund your money."

That's a pantywaist guarantee. Don't even bother advertising it. It's, at best, meh, and at worst, what every halfway decent company should do anyway.

Having a rockin' guarantee assures me of your belief in your product or service. How bold can you be? Can you be as bold as our clients in Milwaukee and Chicago, Penny Mustard Furnishings? Here's theirs':

> *Our Warranty is simple. Our family will take care of your family's furniture to the 8th generation. In tracing our family tree back as far as we could, we determined that a "Generation" in our family was 35 years, 10.5 months. In taking care of our furniture for 8 generations our warranty is 287 years.*
>
> *Simply put, 287 years from now, if your great, great, great, great, great, great grandchild needs service done on your Penny Mustard furniture, our great, great, great, great, great, great grandchild will satisfactorily repair your Penny Mustard furniture or offer to replace it.*

Does any furniture in your house have a 287-year guarantee?

Big, Hairy, Awesome Warranties, Assurances, and Guarantees (BHAWAGs) make for great marketing. They show consumers you're not typical. You're willing to pay a price for greatness.

Create your own BHAWAG:

1. Audit your current warranties, assurances, and guarantees.

2. List out your company's core values.

3. Brainstorm ways to intersect #1 and #2 to exaggerate your offer.

4. If your result doesn't make you, at first, slightly uncomfortable, and then make you puff out your chest, go back to step #3 and retry.

Remember, good messaging isn't born out of flowery writing. It comes from the customer experience born out of brilliant strategy, which includes boldly applying your core values to your systems, your policies, your procedures, your warranties, and your guarantees.

Jack up your warranties. Create BHAWAGs. Be strong. Stand tall by doing the right thing. Your business will grow. I guarantee it.

YOUR CAUSES

The Business of Doing Well by Doing Good

We knew the pendulum began to swing toward coming together to make the world a better place in the late 1990's.

A 2017 workplace survey by Deloitte showed that nearly 9 out of 10 (89 percent) working Americans believe that companies who sponsor volunteer activities offer a better overall working environment than those who do not. In fact, 70 percent of respondents say that volunteer activities are more likely to boost employee morale than company-sponsored happy hours, and 77 percent say, "volunteering is essential to employee well-being."[1]

In a March 2016 article for charities.org, Sarah Ford writes in her lede:

> "What if I told you that having an employee volunteer program could potentially save you money—say $1,000 to $6,000 per employee. Would you start one? Or if you have one, would you take it more seriously?"[2]

But without a plan, many well-meaning businesses fall short of their own goals and desires when it comes to doing good.

If you connect charitable giving with your company's identity (and we think you should), consider implementing a strategic plan for the good-doing efforts of your family business.

You can avoid being reduced to flipping a coin when the phone rings to offer a new sponsorship opportunity by following these simple steps:

1. Set a budget of both time and money. What's your budgeted amount for giving back to your community? Set a dollar amount or a percentage. Build in margin for spontaneous giving. Give credit for volunteering or agree as a company to participate in a certain number of community events each year.

---

1   https://www2.deloitte.com/content/dam/Deloitte/us/Documents/about-deloitte/us-2017-deloitte-volunteerism-survey.pdf

2   https://www.charities.org/news/business-case-employee-volunteer-skills-giving-programs

2. Decide ahead of time what causes, organizations, or communities you will support. Connect to a charity that connects to your business. Do you own a local food store? Consider getting behind the local food bank or backpack buddies program in your community. It helps to connect to a charity that your employees support. How do you know what that is? Just ask them and they will tell you. Or look at their shoes or t-shirts; they may already be telling you.

3. Set up a giving calendar. Will you spread the good throughout the year, or focus it at one time if that will have the biggest impact? If you have this plan in place, it eliminates all those coin-flipping situations.

4. Involve your team. Empower decision-making. Get the team involved by setting up a group volunteer project that everyone can do together.

5. As a successful business leader, put your skills to use on the Board of Directors of your favorite charity. If you have expertise in the areas of finance, human resources, fund development, or marketing (and if you own a family business, you have all those, right?), your time and talent would be a tremendous gift.

6. If all this seems like more than you want to take on, consider joining forces with an existing charity campaign that will do all this for you.

Want to be a well-acting business instead of just a well-meaning business? Make a plan today.

The Cause Clause

Are there systems, policies, and procedures you can tie to your causes? We call these Cause Clauses. Cause Clauses are great ways to accelerate your community impact.

In today's increasingly skeptical world, it's critical to contribute to more than your company's bottom line. How will your company help make your community a better place? What policies will you put into place to do right by others aligned with your core values?

Cause Clauses can take a couple forms:

1. Specific nonprofit community organizations to whom your company donates time, talent, or treasure.

2. Discounts, benefits, or other perks for certain persons or organizations that share your values.

Specific Community Organizations

As much as we'd like, we cannot give to every worthy organization who asks so of us. By consciously choosing a number of events or organizations you'll support, you allow yourself permission to give a gracious "no" to others.

What Organizations Should You Support?

Who shares your values? Who shares family ties? Who deserves it? Ask your staff. Just be sure to do your due diligence that the organization is truly and transparently benefiting your community. If it's a registered 501(c)3 organization, you'll be able to research how much (or how little) of their budget goes toward administrative salaries and overhead and how much (or how little) goes toward the actual service of helping people.

Time? Treasure? Talent?

It's simple to write a check and be done with it, but it's not always the best way to help either the organization or your own company. Sometimes the best thing you can do is schedule a team-building day stuffing backpacks for a local food bank or helping to build a home for Habitat. Other times, it's collecting pennies in a jar or washing cars or holding a competition or some sort. When evaluating who you'll help, remember to give equal consideration to how you'll help them.

Discounts, Benefits, and Other Perks

Steve Holland is a good man and a good friend who owns and operates successful heating, air conditioning, and electrical companies in Milwaukee, Wisconsin. Because of his beliefs, Steve offers an everyday 10% discount to Active Military Personnel and First Responders (police, fire, EMS/EMT). Does he have to do this? No. Is it awesome that he does? Yes. Does it benefit him in the long run? I believe so, but I believe so because he's not doing it for long-term benefit, but rather because he and his wife, Kari, believe it's simply the right thing to do.

You may designate just one month where a portion of your sales go to benefit a certain community organization. This is a gracious and noble gesture, but be sure who you're ultimately trying to benefit. Make sure you're doing it to help the organization and not simply trying to make yourself look good. Sincerity matters, and our insincerity detectors and self-serving meters are blisteringly accurate.

Start by considering which community organizations matter to you and your team, then consider how you'll help those organizations—with time, treasure, talent, or discounts to their organizations. Make them part of your standard operating procedures, and while those community organizations may change from quarter to quarter or year to year, your spirit of modeling community engagement for your employees, your customers, and other business owners will be a part of your Company Constitution forever more.

A Caution about Crowdsourcing Causes

A Pew Research study in May of 2016 says 22% of Americans have contributed to a crowdsourced online fundrasing project. How can you ensure at least some of those 22 out of every 100 Good Samaritans contribute to *your* cause?

After more than two decades of helping businesses choose the right causes, I've learned four very important criteria for ensuring their contributions to those causes are as effective and as efficient as possible:

1. Since that same Pew study showed the majority of donors give less than $50, be specific about where the money is going. Are you raising money to help provide playground equipment for a school? What playground equipment? What school? How much does the slide cost? "Help us purchase a new $2,500 slide for The Classical Academy" is much more powerful than "help us purchase playground equipment."

2. Walk the talk. Match your employees' contributions. Consider matching all contributions.

Don't just tell your team you believe in a cause, show them.

3. Be specific about why this thing helps. Cite statistics about exercise and the benefits of playing outdoors. Appeal emotionally to people's memories of playing outdoors (paint pictures/ give rides). Tell your audience *why* The Classical Academy needs a new slide.

4. Make it as easy possible to give and tell your friends about it. Technology is your friend. There have never been more potential ways for friends and family to give (and get credit for giving if that's their thing) than there are today. What's more, make it super-easy to share your cause. According to online fundraising site GoFundMe, sharing a campaign on Facebook increases donations by 350%!

YOUR TEAM

Your Most Important Customers

Are your employees happy? Heck, does it even matter?

Yep.

According to 2016 research by the Gallup Organization, disengaged workers cost the U.S. economy at least $450,000,000,000 per year.

That's 450 billion ... with a b, bub.

And to put it into your own personal perspective, think about how many people you see on Facebook complaining about:

- Having to go into work

- How quickly the weekend went by

- How they've got to find something better

- How much their co-workers annoy them

And those are just the vocal ones! How many more are quietly checked out?

Yes, some people are simply systemically unhappy, but some companies are also systemically dreary and depressing.

Yet, in both cases, some aren't.

If you'd like a head start, Lydia Dishman wrote "Secrets of America's Happiest Companies" for *Fast Company*.

Dishman writes:

> *"What exactly makes those staffers whistle while they work? CareerBliss just released its findings on the 50 happiest companies in America. The data, based on employee-submitted reviews, evaluated the key factors such as work–life balance, one's relationship with his/her boss and coworkers, work environment, job resources, compensation, growth opportunities, company culture, company reputation, daily tasks, and job control over work performed on a daily basis. The answer to what makes a happy company is an amalgam of all these different factors, which might indicate that companies perceived as innovative would consistently snag the top spots. Not so."*

How about you? Any advice? What does your company do? What do you do?

Hollywood has cashed in on employee unhappiness via the likes of *Office Space* and *The Office*, and the popularity of these movies and shows proves just how unhappy the American workforce is. And as we mentioned earlier, you see living proof of it daily when you read your friends' Facebook statuses. People complain so much about their jobs that the act of whining becomes a full-time job in itself.

Reach for the Top

Still not convinced it's worth it to cater to your employees? Research shows that the 100 best companies to work for are also among the most profitable. No one's going to deny the success of Google and Edward Jones, and they both rank in the top 10.

There's no reason you can't mimic this success on a smaller scale. Offer to pay for flu shots. Give exceptional employee discounts. Keep a small pantry stocked with healthy, tasty snacks for anyone to graze on. If you know your business well, it won't be hard to find easy and affordable perks.

If your internal customers feel engaged and taken care of, this positive energy will transfer to your external customers. Your employees are your clients' first point of human contact. Make them a successful part of what you do and watch them help your customers with a smile worth a million bucks.

HOW TO BUILD A CULTURE OF OWNERSHIP

Are Your Employees VIP Customers?

In a massive company, employees' roles are precise: accountant, marketing manager, IT support specialist, and so on. In a corporation, an IT support specialist isn't likely to be called upon to do the books. In a small business, however, the manager might find herself cleaning up after the popular shop cat, because every employee of a small business has to wear multiple hats.

The most important hat your employees wear is the customer hat—now available in "extremely satisfied." That's right. Your employees are also your customers, and they should be treated as VIPs.

Understand Who Your Customers Are

Even though you're not running a large corporation, you can still split your customer base into "internal" and "external." Your external customers are the obvious, visible ones. They pay you money for products or services.

Your internal customers are your employees; they're the ones who keep the external customers coming in the door. It's a direct link: If your employees aren't enthusiastic about where they work, it's unlikely they'll be able to create a pleasant experience that external customers will want to come back to.

Keep All Your Customers Happy

You need to strive to keep your employees as happy as you want your customers to be. Remember that, even during tough economic times, employees, like customers, still have options. If they are choosing to work for you, make it worth their while.

Scott Thompson, CFO of independent contemporary Christian radio station in Columbus, OH, 104.9 The River, has a simple leadership strategy for keeping everyone happy. According to Thompson, "The leader's role is simply to create an environment where his employees can do their best work, evaluate that work, and reward the results of that work." That's it: create, evaluate, reward.

A Culture of Ownership

One of the best ways to create a staff-friendly environment is to make your employees a true, indispensable part of your business. This creates a culture of ownership where everyone feels engaged. Here are some things worth trying:

1. Share everything: financials, goals, failures, and achievements.

2. Ask for input, and then follow through.

3. Listen more than you talk.

4. Reward employees, and also hold them accountable.

5. Get your hands dirty. You won't win the respect of your staff without doing what they do every now and then.

Far beyond simply making Friday "Hawaiian Shirt Day," a culture of ownership means that when your business hurts, the whole staff hurts, and when it wins, everyone wins. If employees feel involved, they will be enthusiastic and successful when dealing with your client base.

Hire for Values

Want to increase your company's value? Hire for values.

If a tentative hire makes it through an interview and her resume checks out, take her to dinner.

After those first couple of interviews, you're going to have a pretty good idea of a potential hire's technical knowledge.

But you need to share a meal with the potential hire to get a better sense of her or his values.

Review your own values and center the dinner conversations around questions that might demonstrate examples of your company values.

You want to make sure she's a good fit. You won't just be doing everyone in your company a favor. You'll be doing her a favor as well.

Success happens when all employees share values and work toward the same goals.

Is it any wonder our most successful clients' market shares are starting to blow past what every expert we know and trust suggests they should be able to do?

With a strong foundation of shared goals and values, the sky's the limit.

HOW TO GET GREAT PERFORMANCES

In Lee Cockerell's *Creating Magic*, he writes about leadership strategies he helped to create at Disney, and he gives the million-dollar question for any business owner.

Ask your employees:

"IS ANYTHING STANDING IN THE WAY OF GREAT PERFORMANCE?"

Cockerell writes:

> "[Ask them] whether it's sluggish procedures, unclear operating guidelines, obsolete equipment, inadequate training, etc. Then ask if there is something you can do to make their jobs easier. Listen intently, write down what they tell you, and follow up quickly by fixing the problem."

Remember, as an owner, manager, or leader of your company, your most important customers are your employees. Schedule time to personally ask this question to each of your employees.

And make sure to follow through.

For them to do their jobs at the highest level, you must first do yours at the highest level.

They need you to give a great performance. Ask them today... then ask them again next week... and the week after...

GIVE THE GIFT-OF-ALL-GIFTS TO YOUR TEAM

It was Troy Jansen's idea, and we have his permission to share it, and you have his permission to borrow it.

This handwritten piece of paper is affixed majestically to the inside of the bathroom door at Jansen's Heating & Air in Effingham, Illinois.

Yes, that Effingham, Illinois... famous for America's largest cross, a Ben Folds' song, and Jansen's Heating & Air, of which Troy is now the General Manager.

Troy had made a list of every team member's natural gifts and talents and listed them where he knew every person would see them, uhh, regularly.

This gift-of-all-gifts cost him nothing but his time, but what a treasure to his team.

You could do the same today... or print out a copy of this post for your boss and majestically affix it somewhere you know she or he might see it...

Just a thought... we don't know about you, but we do some of our best thinking... would you like to see it?

Turn the page.

Tom — Knowledgeable - We all know he has the answer or can get it

Cindy — Caring - Always looking after everyone's best interest.

Kayla — Creative- Your mind blowing w/ your pace & great ideas

Jessica — Accomodating- Willing to work with everyone & each department

Jenna — Team Focus- Being in Pasa You Still Always Have The Whole Team In Mind

Kristen — Customer Focus- No customer slips through the cracks.

Jerry — Well Informed- Always up to date & willing to help.

Jim — Communicative- Always Positive & Helping People Smile.

Tim S — Stunning- Your Sales & New Ideas Are Amazing.

Andy — Smart- If it's a technical issue, You can always help fix it.

Leon — Skilled- Your Experience is Priceless.

Trent — Challenging- Always Challenging Everyone To Be Better.

Dave — Steady-You have your way that works great & it's always the same

Matt M — Receptive- Willing to accept challenges & advice

Ryan — Dedicated- You truly Love your new position as a Service Tech

Dennis — Strategic- You Always Have A Plan & Willingness to help others.

Tim J — Tireless- You wear many hats & always get things done.

Dan — Thought Provoking- Always thinking of new ideas & processes.

Eric — Quick Witted- Not Just By Poking At Dan, You'll tackle anything

Matt S — Responsive- Very quick learner & will always

RETAINING THE BEST PLAYERS ON YOUR TEAM: MOSS KANTER, MASLOW, & THREE MOTIVATORS MORE IMPORTANT THAN MONEY

Increased employee engagement leads directly to increased employee loyalty. When it comes to employee loyalty, did you know there are three motivators more important than money?

That's according to Harvard Business School Professor Rosabeth Moss Kanter, who's pretty much the smartest person on the planet when it comes to employee loyalty. You might want to listen to her.

The three before money? Also M's, according to Professor Moss Kanter...

MEMBERSHIP: Create community by honoring individuality. Employees have a strong desire to feel like part of a team.

MASTERY: Help people develop deep skills. Employees have a strong desire to learn new skills and feel accomplished.

MEANING: Repeat and reinforce a larger purpose. Employees have a strong desire to be striving toward some greater good.

Therefore, as you brainstorm ways to reward employees and increase motivation and employee loyalty, consider what projects, training, and team activities you could use to celebrate milestones in your company.

Interestingly, and Professor Moss Kanter doesn't mention this in any of her research as far as we know, these motivators correspond nicely with Abraham Maslow's Hierarchy of Needs. Maslow taught us that humans are perpetually wanting creatures, and he illustrated it in the pyramid on the next page.

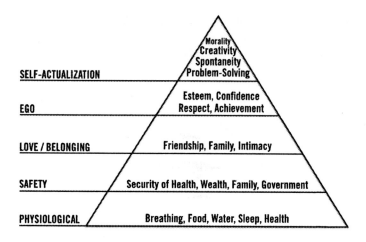

Once one level is met, you ascend to another, and we are always striving to reach the next level.

Isn't it interesting, then, that Professor Moss Kanter's three M's each ascends a level higher into Maslow's Hierarchy?

Money's required for the first two levels to provide basic needs. Membership provides for psychological belonging and love needs. Mastery satisfies our psychological need for prestige and feelings of accomplishment.

And finally, meaning... and humankind's search for it... satisfies the very highest order of Maslow's hierarchy.

Dude. It's science.

In other words, two really, really smart people—and our team—are saying you need to strongly consider recalibrating how you motivate your team.

What steps will you take to do so? When? If not, why not?

WHY IN THE WORLD WOULD YOU GIVE US YOUR BEST STUFF IN A BOOK???

Because, by and large, 50+ combined years of experience with uncovering these things about a family business have taught our firm how to connect their dots and see dots others don't even see.

It's our hope that by sharing this information, three things will happen:

1. Thousands of businesses will begin to learn how to build a solid foundation for present and future success regardless of shifts in technology and the endless onslaught of the new, "best" media channels.

2. Good companies will know we mean what we say when we admit our recruitment model is based on teaching incredibly valuable information for free.

3. Some of those good companies will recognize their own values in ours and call us up to learn what else we know and how we can tailor it to their specific family business.

Our company is paid on growth. We charge a flat monthly fee that's adjusted annually by how much you grow. The only way for us to make more money is to help you grow your business. How's that for a confident guarantee? What sort of guarantees with teeth do you provide?

HOW TO TURN STRATEGIC PLANNING INTO STRATEGIC DOING

It's an old cliché: "What gets measured, gets done."

Sure. Fine. We have a truer one for you:

"You improve what you measure *and reward.*"

Repeat that aloud... and do NOT lop off that last part about rewarding.

NOW, CREATE YOUR COMPANY CONSTITUTION

If the Declaration of Independence was, in addition to being our country's declaration of war, a statement of its values, then our Constitution was the list of systems, policies, and procedures (laws) America would use to manifest and secure those values.

By using the resources in this chapter, you've now learned the ten most common limiting factors:

1. Business Model

2. Walking the Talk

3. Your Market Potential & Share

4. Your Competition

5. Your Marketing Budgets

6. Your Customers

7. Your Blind Spots

8. Your Warranties, Assurances, and Guarantees

9. Your Causes

10. Your Team

So, what are we going to do with all this stuff? You're going to work with your team to create a Company Constitution that outlines your systems, policies, and procedures that are all motivated by one of your company's core values and help to accomplish the goals you listed in your 20/2/0 vision.

It's a document that will evolve over time as you revise your two-year objectives, but this document should be priority #1 for new hires: *Read this. Understand this.*

It should be a sequence of beliefs motivated by values that manifest themselves in observable actions either to your team or your customers. You're creating the strategy that dictates how you delight your customers using the very DNA of your company—your core values—to help you achieve your goals that were carefully chosen to help you complete your mission. Know what else? You're also creating a clear standard of company culture and the collective criteria by which employees will be hired, fired, and will or will not advance. You're saying:

THESE ARE THINGS THAT ARE IMPORTANT TO US. ARE THEY IMPORTANT TO YOU?

As a leader of your company, you're responsible for stewarding the company culture. This document serves as a covenant of the founding principles of that culture. Hold it sacred and review it regularly. Your annual retreat is a perfect time to review your Company Constitution and add or remove any observable actions or values or alter the mission if your team's in agreement. Even our Constitution is amended from time to time.

By doing all this heavy lifting in the first two foundational tiers of The First Order of Business, you've made it super-super-super simple to audit and optimize your customer experience and provide truly Shareworthy Customer Service... which is the focus of our next level of The First Order of Business!

IN THE WORKBOOK VERSION OF BRAND YOUR OWN BUSINESS, WE PROVIDE 51 PAGES OF EXERCISES TO HELP YOU AND YOUR TEAM WITH STRATEGIC PLANNING AND CRAFTING YOUR COMPANY CONSTITUTION.

TO ORDER OR LEARN MORE ABOUT THE BYOB WORKBOOK, VISIT:

BRANDYOUROWN.BUSINESS

Breathe. You're awesome.

> *Your customers hold you to a high standard. If you want to achieve true excellence, raise that bar even higher for yourself, your colleagues, and everyone around you.*

LEE COCKERELL

March
2013

SECTION THREE

CUSTOMER EXPERIENCE

DID YOU KNOW THE SECOND WEEK IN OCTOBER IS NATIONAL CUSTOMER SERVICE WEEK?

This isn't just some gimmick. It's a presidentially decreed gimmick. Back in 1992, when President George H. W. Bush first proclaimed National Customer Service Week, he urged "all Americans to observe this week with appropriate programs and activities."

This raises several questions:

1. What are these "appropriate programs and activities" for National Customer Service Week?

2. Does this mean there are *inappropriate* programs and activities?

3. Why do we even need National Customer Service Week?

Yes, the purpose of national commemorative days and weeks is to bring awareness to a large number of worthy (and a few not-so-worthy) causes. And, yes, customer service should be integrated, calculated, and celebrated.

But with all due respect, President Bush, one week just ain't gonna cut it.

Therefore, we proclaim it Customer Service Year! We urge you to celebrate all year by implementing some of the programs, ideas, and plans in this section of the book.

Then, when the year is up, repeat.

There's a big difference between committing to one week a year and committing a year.

One week = lethal. Every year = legendary.

Customer Service Year doesn't begin January 1st. It begins when you want it to begin.

Today's a good day. Celebrate responsibly.

THREE LESSONS FROM A GOOD COMCAST SERVICE STORY

It's like the company-that-shall-not-be-named... its very utterance puffs cheeks and turns faces red.

The "C" word... is NOT for use in civil conversation.

Consistently ranked one of the most hated companies in America (Google "Comcast worst company America" and you'll more than 200,000 results, but hey! Great news for Comcast: According to *Consumerist*, they're no longer the absolute worst of the worst), they're famous for disappointing customers.

Truth is, Comcast has millions of customers, and we hear only a select few stories of outrage. The rage/customer ratio is likely low, but when we hear about their disappointing customer service, boy, do we hear about it!

That's your first lesson.

Squeaky wheels demand grease, and when they don't get greased, they squeak louder and louder and louder. Social media has provided them with an amplifier of unprecedented volume and duration. Stories of poor customer service last forever.

Want to go viral? Disappoint a customer.

In a 2013 study, Accenture found angry customers cost companies $5.9 trillion. That's $5,900,000,000,000!

The Second Lesson

Happy customers are, by and large, content customers... meaning, they're not anywhere near as likely to leave reviews as unhappy customers.

This is just as true for your company as it is for Comcast, though not to such a large degree.

Do you have a process in place for (a) asking for reviews, and (b) making it easy for your customers to leave you reviews?

How can you reduce the friction between your customer and a good, great, or breathtakingly awesome review?

The Third—and Most Important—Lesson

Why was our experience with Comcast so good?

We had paid to upgrade our Internet. Our business does, on average, a dozen video conferences each week, and it's a necessary expense for us to have a huge, heaping pile of bandwidth to push and pull those audio and video signals in their best possible resolution. It's a currency of our credibility.

Without getting too technical, we were getting "okay fast" Internet (100 Mbps down / 20 up), but (thanks to new competition) they were offering "paisley speed" Internet (250 Mbps down/40 up), and it was perfect for us.

We called Comcast service, and the technician came to our home, and it soon became clear it wasn't a simple process for him. Something was wrong.

What happened over the next two hours was the lesson.

Our problem... became *his* problem.

He was more frustrated than us. He owned that problem, and he did not quit until he had found a solution. This required him to test and try a couple hours worth of solutions. He tested every link in the chain, and he stayed until he could look us in the eye and assure us he'd fixed what needed fixed.

It involved poor wiring outside our home and a bad modem inside our home.

He did so without complaint; he did so with Sherlockian enthusiasm.

Wasn't he just doing his job?

Sure. You could certainly say that with truth... and leave it at that...

But Comcast is (in)famous for not "just doing their job," aren't they? They pass more bucks than a Johnson County, Illinois, deer processing stand. And that's one of my problems:

There is no "they." Comcast is a company of mostly hard-working, diligent, caring people, just like your company.

One of those people came to our home and made our problem his problem.

That sense of ownership—his not saying "Well, you're going to need to talk to someone else at Comcast," or some such thing—is what we took away from our experience with his company.

Do your employees own their customers' problems?

Do they do so without complaint?

Do they attack those problems with Sherlockian curiosity, intensity, and relentlessness?

Do you reward them for doing so?

See... that might be Comcast's problem... or one of them...

Did we leave them a review?

Nope. They never asked. (See also: The Second Lesson)

Hopefully one day, Comcast will ask us about *Brand Your Own Business*.

BEST BUY MADE OUR MOM CRY

Our mom's not a crier. She's kind, hard-working, helpful, and thoughtful. She volunteers at a local clinic, reads books, cooks, and gardens. She is not technologically savvy. She does not cry.

Best Buy made our mom cry.

Is it any wonder reports of their slow demise litter the inter webs?

Okay, technically the corporation didn't make our mom cry. Trish did.

Trish—of the Geek Squad—at a central Illinois location. We're not redacting her last name just to be polite. We just don't know it. If we did, we'd include it, along with her home phone, address, Social Security number, PIN #, blood type, and known allergies.

After years of good customer service with the Geek Squad—and a very pleasant and apologetic follow-up from someone else after Poop Face Trish brought our mom to tears—it took only one bad experience for Mom to tell us and for us to tell you.

Companies across the world pour billions of dollars into marketing and advertising, and it's met with—at best—mixed results.

In this era of interconnectivity, where we're all just a text, tweet, post, video, or picture away, how many companies are devoting serious marketing dollars to enhancing the customer experience? Or, sadly, should we ask, how few?

What if, instead, companies focused on building Shareworthy Customer Service systems of implementing, measuring, and rewarding efforts of customer delight? What if those companies budgeted for it?

We know some do, right? We know Disney and Apple and Ritz-Carlton and Nordstrom's all empower and reward their teams for customer satisfaction and delight. Is it any coincidence those companies are filling our Facebook news feeds with pictures and stories of happy children and smiling customers?

And there's a dark side of Shareworthy Customer Service, too, isn't there? What else floods our feeds? Stories of contempt and employee apathy and injustice. Speaking of which... Trish? If we find out where you live, we're putting spiders in your air vents and snakes in your bed.

WHAT IS SHAREWORTHY CUSTOMER SERVICE? YOU TELL US.

Who has the most out-of-this-world customer service in your city?

If you're like 80% of people asked that question, no one comes to mind.

Yes, that's sad.

It's also an opportunity, but before you can be that company, you need a frame of reference. How much do you pay attention to customer service? You need to start.

Wanna do something interesting this weekend?

If you want to begin to understand what truly delightful Shareworthy Customer Service is, you need to become mindful of, and even critically think about, customer delight.

Shareworthy Customer Service can be simply defined as *service so spectacularly good (or bad) that you share it with your friends, your family, and your social networks.*

THIS WEEKEND? KEEP SCORE.

Keep a notebook (we call ours a "mindfulness diary") with you this weekend—or use an app on your smartphone—and keep track of every interaction you have with companies... at the bank, at restaurants, at gas stations.

When you have a noteworthy experience, think about why it was noteworthy. Deconstruct what made it great or bad.

Ask your team to do the same.

On Monday, get together and compare and contrast.

But don't be surprised when most of your experiences sink into the pit of mediocrity— which has never been wider or deeper.

ARE YOU FALLING INTO THE PIT OF MEDIOCRITY?

We hear about the extraordinary. We share the extraordinary.

We hear about the nasty mung of awful. We share horror stories of said nasty mung.

It's a dangerous wasteland, my friends. It's a narcotic malaise that deadens souls of employees, companies, and customers.

And it's true for most of the companies we do business with.

That's the thing about extremes: for better and for worse, they get covered. And even when a company stinks up the place, it usually gets at least one chance to make good, and that chance, if taken advantage of, tends to get as much coverage as the offense. We do love our redemptions, don't we?

But what about the rest?

Ugh.

Imagine an inverted bell curve.

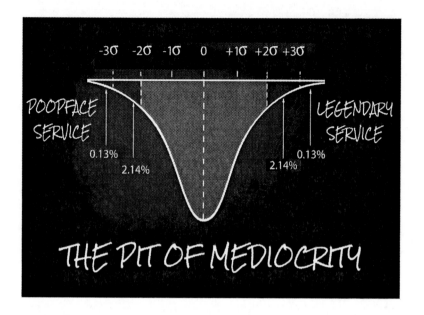

The Pit of Mediocrity

At both extremes, you get discussed.

There, in the saggy, soggy bottom, sits a black-hole-suck it's hard to escape from. Why would you try to escape when you don't think there's a problem?

"Our service is fine."

"We do a pretty good job."

"Hey, we're good. When we make a mistake, we always try to fix it."

When the status quo has overtaken your company, your employees may not know—or no longer remember—how your values and goals combine to define your purpose that manifests itself through the observable systems, policies, and procedures that dictate a delightful, intentional customer experience.

Maybe it's time to shake up the tank a little bit.

WHO REALLY CARES? ASK DUNBAR.

Who cares? 148.7 people, apparently.

That's what Robin Dunbar, director of the Institute of Cognitive and Evolutionary Anthropology of the University of Oxford, calculated as the cognitive limit of the number of people with whom we can maintain meaningful friendships.

Dunbar's Number has ramifications in social media, sure, but for family business, it has far more to do with marketing and influence and the importance of delivering a delightful customer experience, and echoing that experience and your company's values in your messaging.

Humans rarely make decisions in a vacuum. Each of us is guided by co-workers, family members, neighbors, and friends.

If you are typical and healthy, you maintain about 150 people in your "realm of association." Some of these are permanent members of that realm, while others will pass through your life and be replaced. But the number hovers at about 150. And guess what? Beyond their connection to you, these 150 people have little, if anything, in common. They are your personal world: the male and female, young and old, rich and poor, white-collar and blue-collar "masses" that give your life purpose and meaning.

You are someone's target customer. If we fail to reach you with our ads but our company is beloved by half the people in your realm of association, what's the likelihood that you'll hear about it?

Google and Facebook, radio and television, magazines and mailers, and billboards and flyers are called mass media because they reach the masses. The ability to "target" using mass media is more illusion than fact.

We're here today to tell you to deliver a powerful experience and echo that experience and your company's values in your message campaigns.

And if every employee of your company can delight just one customer per day, and each of those customers share their awesome experiences with their 148.7, that's hundreds, thousands, or even millions of positive impressions *per day*! Dude, it's science!

So, why not make those experiences awesome?

WHAT DOES ALL THIS HAVE TO DO WITH ADVERTISING?

Advertising only accelerates the inevitable.

Good advertising will make a good business more successful more quickly and more efficiently.

Good advertising will make a bad business go out of business faster.

If you're in between, languishing in the Pit of Mediocrity, you'll try advertising, and it won't work very well (if at all, depending on a few factors)— at least, not nearly as well as it could.

Advertising messages fail for two reasons:

1. Companies don't speak to consumers about things consumers care about in a language consumers understand.

2. Companies don't live up to the promises they make in their advertising.

Believe it or not, it's easier to hire a really good ad writer to avoid failing because of reason #1. It's much harder for a business to avoid failure for reason #2.

That's why it's so important. That's why you'll be so successful when you implement Shareworthy Customer Service.

SIMPLIFYING SHAREWORTHY CUSTOMER SERVICE

The Reverend Harold T. Mooney taught me to love God and golf. He was able to simplify both for me.

When we'd talk about golf at the driving range or in the big emerald yard behind the church, he'd say, "Tim, so many people want to confuse the issue with thoughts of movements and swing and where the left wrist should be at impact. It gets your brain so full, it's impossible to perform."

"Simplify the game down to what matters," he said. "Two things—study two things, think about two things, practice two things, and you'll learn to master the game."

"Golf," Fr. Mooney said, "comes down to direction and distance. Nothing more or less."

ALS, Lou Gehrig's Disease, took one of my heroes much too quickly, but I remember the lesson, Father.

After researching hundreds of stories, reading a half-dozen books and interviewing a few world-class company leaders, I've realized—as I'm sure you have—that recognizing delightful and spectacular customer service isn't really all that hard.

In fact, the same 14 characteristics that seem to define magnificent and remarkable customer service pop up time and again in story after story.

But so did something else. Another pattern emerged after a couple hundred hours of research—something even simpler.

While there are 14 manifestations, 14 defining characteristics, 14 ways to deliver delight, those 14 fall evenly into two halves.

We'll give you all 14 in the following chapters, plus a lesson in how to implement them, but before we go there, we want to simplify customer service down to what matters.

Study these two things.

Think about these two things.

Practice these two things, and you'll learn to master the game.

After researching hundreds of stories, two common threads tie them all together:

1.   Professionalism

2.   Kindness

Each has seven links that shoot off to deliver these characteristics to the customer, but if you wish to boil it down to the basic building blocks of all Shareworthy

Customer Service stories, it's those two, bub: Professionalism and Kindness.

We told you it was simple. Just like golf, it's simple to read about or watch—the greats make it look so effortless, don't they? The Apples and the Disneys and the Zapposeseses.

Heck, it's even relatively easy to start to play the game yourself, isn't it?

But mastery ... going pro? Well ... it's, frankly, just as simple.

It's just not easy.

THE 14 FACETS OF SHAREWORTHY CUSTOMER SERVICE

We've spent countless hours researching studies and stories of customer service. We've read the horror stories, and we've heard the stories of spectacular, Shareworthy Customer Service.

We're sure you have your own stories in both corners.

As we researched, patterns emerged. It's pretty neat, actually—over hundreds of stories, we couldn't find anything that didn't fit the pattern.

Think of the foundation of Shareworthy Customer Service as two big honkin' rocks—each with seven facets.

Big Honkin' Rock #1: Professionalism

1. Appearance

2. Attentiveness

3. Dependability

4. Consistency

5. Focus

6. Proactivity

7. Simplicity

Big Honkin' Rock #2: Kindness

1. Active Listening

2. Empathy

3. Engagement

4. Memory

5. Manners

6. Playfulness

7. Privilege

There you go. Those are the heavy seven plus seven.

THE 7 FACETS OF PROFESSIONALISM

Kindness (or its absence) makes a world of difference, but it's relatively meaningless without first rocking Professionalism. Kindness is the sexy component but these seven facets of Professionalism drive the bus.

APPEARANCE

Whether it's never seeing trash at Disney or your heating and air conditioning technician slipping floor savers over his shoes, we notice the look, sound, and smell of the persons, places, and things we do business with.

Even if the coffee house hipster barista sports her skinny jeans and Residents t-shirt, we still expect a certain degree of cleanliness and order to her rumples. The same holds true for your parking lot, your service vans, and your bathroom.

ATTENTIVENESS

Look me in the eye. Acknowledge you've seen me and are preparing to engage with me. When it's my turn, don't excuse me for the person calling on the phone.

In his book *EntreLeadership*, Dave Ramsey tells the story of the pizza delivery driver who watched his tips increase when he began jogging from his car to the door. Make us feel like we matter. It's really not that hard. We have to do business with each other anyway, so the quicker you can help me, the quicker I'll be out of your life.

DEPENDABILITY

Can we count on you to do what you say you're going to do when you say you're going to do it? Typically, an absence of dependability becomes Shareworthy—and not in a good way.

CONSISTENCY

Consistency is the dependability of your dependability. You need systems, policies, and procedures to deliver dependability, umm, dependably.

FOCUS

A customer at hand isn't just an important thing—it's the only thing that matters at any given moment. The best servers in restaurants have this down, don't they? She might have 15 tables, but you'd never know it.

Restaurant owner Laura Harbaugh called it "The 3-Second Rule."

"I may be speaking with you only for three seconds. But for those three seconds, I'm locked in. You are the only thing that matters to me in the world."

It's harder than ever amid the growing distractions. It's also more important than ever.

PROACTIVITY

We originally had nine facets of each main component, but realized a couple were pretty much the same (we had "proactivity" and "authority"), so we narrowed them down.

Here's an example of Authority: Any Ritz Carlton employee can comp up to $100 worth of services to make something right on the spot. The best business owners train their employees, then give them the authority to make decisions the owner will support even when they don't necessarily agree with it.

As previously mentioned, read Carl Sewell's *Customers For Life* if you want to learn more about this.

SIMPLICITY

Technological, ahem, advances have helped companies build walls in the name of "customer convenience."

Please. Did any customer ever ask for an automated phone tree? The layers of complexity in today's work and world increase friction. We're faster, busier, multi-tasking, aggressive, noisy creatures that demand attention NOW.

Shareworthy Customer Service providers have a gift of being able to evaluate a complex situation and quickly distill it down and remove any tension or friction. You can just feel tense situations deflate at Apple's Genius Bars when a 22-year-old uses common language to describe an otherwise technical problem to a 75-year-old laptop owner. Watch a great guest services manager in Las Vegas hear a problem, understand a problem, and fix a problem quickly and quietly.

There you go. Those are the first heavy seven.

How does your company rate with each? Do you actually have systems and policies in place to point these facets in your favor, or are y'all just winging it?

THE 7 FACETS OF KINDNESS

We just examined the Seven Facets of Professionalism—the boring bedrocks of any successful company. Now we get to talk about Professionalism's fun baby sister: Kindness.

Kindness gets all the headlines and wins all the awards. Kindness is splashy and silly and three-exclamation-point-all-caps FUN!!!

ACTIVE LISTENING

You can usually tell when people are dialed in, can't you? Active listening changes your expression. Your head leans forward, and you fidget less—if at all. You're really hearing someone's problem, challenge, or situation. It builds confidence in the person telling the story.

You can dazzle them by repeating back the essence of what they said "just to make sure you have it right." So many people today don't listen actively. They seem to be merely waiting for the other person to finish so they can start talking again. Sound familiar? The good news is that you can practice your active listening skills every day.

EMPATHY

The simple truth is: The customer isn't always right. Shocking? Not really, when you consider the customer rarely has all the information you have. An expert at empathy understands the delicate bridge connecting what the customer thinks they want and what the customer truly needs. Put yourself in the customer's shoes, then use the benefit of your expertise to simply show them what they'd really prefer to do if they had your knowledge and skill set.

ENGAGEMENT

Engaged people give off a contagious energy. Your company's next superstar is out there right now willing to dazzle you with his or her eyes and smile and personality. You may just have to pull up to the second window to find her.

A mentor named Dave Wisniewski taught us this tip a long time ago: Keep some cards with you. If you get engaging service at a drive-thru, for example, hand the engager a card and suggest they come in to interview for a sales position with your company.

Think about it—if someone can greet you with bright eyes and a smile at the drive-thru window of Long John Silver's— imagine what she could do making eight to ten times that much without her clothes having to, umm, smell like that every day. You know engaged people when you see them. You know the bright eyes and the locked-in, nothing-else-matters-but-you look.

MEMORY

Make a point—an effort—to remember the names of people's children and what they've been working on lately. Remember a person's favorite drink or what kind of foods they don't like. Little details like these show you care.

If you struggle with remembering, why not use something like Evernote or some other sync-able application to make notes of them? That's how your stylist does it, you know.

MANNERS

Our father, a Marine, and our mother, raised in a family surrounded by schoolteachers, taught us "yes, sir" and "yes ma'am" values at a very early age. We'd rather you tell us our children are polite and respectful than that they're smart or talented or good looking. There's simply no substitute for respect.

PLAYFULNESS

Lord, give us both the ability to take things seriously and the ability to be silly and fun. And please, Lord, give us the wisdom to know when each is appropriate. We ask you, though, wouldn't it be far more remarkable for a place to loosen up and have a little fun more often? Wouldn't most interactions with most businesses be improved with a little fun?

PRIVILEGE

We like to be made to feel special. We like perks and treats and the perception that we're getting some degree of preferential treatment—even if it's policy. For example, when staying at the Vdara hotel in Vegas, I called down to the front desk, and the front desk guy said:

"Hello, Mr. Miles. This is Stephen. How can I help you this evening?"

Look, I know my name pops up on a screen. I don't care. I feel like Elvis. I know the next guy who calls—his name is popping up on the same screen. I don't care. I fall for it every time. It's the little things. Vegas is a fine hub for Shareworthy Customer Service. So are many resorts in the Caribbean. We'd all do well to do some research in one or both of those places, don't you think?

We'll ask again: How does your company rate with each? Do you actually have systems and policies in place to point these facets in your favor, or are y'all just winging it?

IMPLEMENTING SHAREWORTHY CUSTOMER SERVICE

As always, we will continue to increase our marketing budget as a percentage of sales, but we will be lowering our advertising budget.

Huh?

For years, owner-operated companies spent bazillions on things like the Yellow Pages—pouring buckets of cash into the last refuge for people who have no preference.

Now, many of those same companies are using some of that money to buy bags of magic beans from social media experts.

Don't get us wrong. Social media's a fantastic tool for listening and deepening a relationship and doing research and addressing customer concerns and sharing videos of singing dogs and stuff. It's just not a broadcast or direct response medium. It's terrible—for most owner operated companies—at direct response.

So our clients are participating in a grand and frightening experiment. We're going to begin taking part of our ad budget and putting it back into our company's best customers: our employees. Instead we'll be including it in our aforementioned customer retention budget.

Why? You cannot improve what you do not measure and reward. Most managers love the measure part, but they turn the other way and whistle when you remind them about reward. Pity.

To implement this program, we started by asking these best customers—our employees—questions about their ideal rewards, large and small. To get them to buy into this new way of thinking of themselves as being an extension of the marketing department, we have to start by painting a picture of what's in it for them. Each of them has a different carrot at the end of the stick. If we do our job correctly, we'll be able to reward them mightily.

Do you know what your team—your best customers— wants, needs, and desires? We don't mean "more money." We mean specifics. Each one.

Does it bother you that you don't know?

Then, you have to ask them more questions—you have to ask them questions about what would cause a customer to want to share an experience with your company.

You have to ask them about Professionalism and Kindness. What do the defining characteristics of each one look and feel like to your customers? You have to ask them for specifics.

You have to pull out worksheets with the 14 Facets of Shareworthy Customer Service and ask these most important customers of yours how each one could be dialed up with your company's customers. Ask each employee. First, ask them not to share answers so you can see individual results. Then do it again and collaborate on answers.

You need to ask your employees what YOU can do to deliver Shareworthy Customer Service to them. What do they need from you? What resources can you provide them to help them help your customers? After all, they are your best customers.

You're going to have to ask them.

Then, how can you measure and reward these tactics? If you have a Shareworthy Customer Service contest, what are the ground rules?

You know who needs to set them? Your best customers— your employees—they need to OWN IT. They are uniquely qualified to be specific about definitions, systems of measurement, rewards big and small, and implementation.

A funny thing's going to happen on the way to this new world. You're all going to have a heck of a lot of fun along the way. You're really, really going to enjoy coming to work every day and sharing stories of your own.

We're going to continue advertising, don't get me wrong. We're just going to focus on media that allow us to harness the powers of emotion and story. And those stories aren't going to be about margin-killing. Groupon? Eat it, Groupon.

Customer service is the new accelerant. Most companies say they need a Facebook page. Why? They'd be better off focusing on delivering service worth sharing.

You want more likes?

Great. Give people something to actually, you know, like.

MEASURING SHAREWORTHY CUSTOMER SERVICE

How likely is it that your customers would recommend buying from you?

How likely is it that your employees would recommend working for you?

Ask them using the world's shortest, bestest, most awesomest survey–NPS.

What Is NPS?

The open-source Net Promoter Score was invented by Fred Reichheld to measure loyalty, and it's now used by pretty much every company you think of when you think of boss customer service: Apple, Southwest Airlines, Trader Joe's, Zappos, Amazon, and the list goes on and on.

While these companies pay a great deal of money to have their Net Promoter Scores independently surveyed, analyzed, and verified, you can use it yourself for nothing.

It works with customers, employees, donors, volunteers—any group you'd like to build loyalty with.

These three simple questions can be asked by phone, mail, email, or using online software:

1. On a scale of 0 (not likely to recommend) to 10 (extremely likely to recommend), how likely is it that you'd recommend our company to a friend or colleague?

2. What's the biggest reason for your answer to question one?

The third question is conditional, and you can set up an online survey as such.

3. If your answer to question one was not a 10, what do we have to do next time to earn a 10?

That's it! Easy peasy, George and Weezie.

How Is NPS Calculated?

To calculate your NPS score, you use only the answers to question one. Depending on their answer to that question, each respondent falls into one of three categories:

- DETRACTORS gave you a score between 0 and 6.

- PASSIVES gave you a score of 7 or 8.

- PROMOTERS gave you a score of 9 or 10.

Your score will be a hard number (as opposed to a percentage) between zero and one hundred.

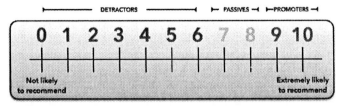

PROMOTERS%−DETRACTORS% = NPS

An Example Of Net Promoter Score (NPS)

Let's say you surveyed 100 customers this week:

61 gave you a 9 or 10.

30 gave you a 7 or 8.

9 gave you somewhere between 0 and 6.

First, calculate your promoter percentage: 61/100 or 61%.

Then, calculate your detractor percentage: 9/100 or 9%.

Subtract your detractor percentage from the promoter percentage (61−9) to arrive at your NPS of 52.

Is 52 Any Good?

Sure! Remember, this isn't an elementary school grading scale. You didn't fail. You'd lead some industries with a score of 52.

This is a big opportunity to examine your strategic plan for customer delight. Your score isn't the end. It's only the beginning.

Why Is NPS the BestBestBest?

It's easy to take. Recently, I had United Airlines ask me to take a non-NPS customer survey. They told me it would take approximately 25-35 minutes. Who has time for that? By contrast, NPS can be completed in as few as two seconds. Even if someone fills out all three answers, it shouldn't take her more than five minutes.

It's easy to understand. In addition to brevity, NPS wins with clarity. We've used zero to ten scales forever. We understand them. We also know what it means to recommend someone to a friend.

It's easy for a business to follow through. Questions two and three provide immediate, direct feedback to a business from their customers. Not only can you see patterns emerge, but you can also reach out to customers directly to address problems and close feedback loops. In the example above, you could reach out directly to the nine detractors to solve their issues. Then, you could start to work on the thirty passives.

Take Action!

You can—and should—regularly ask the same of your employees. You can use question #1 verbatim or ask it differently, saying:

On a scale of 0 (not likely to recommend) to 10 (extremely likely to recommend), how likely is it that you'd recommend working for (our company) to a friend or colleague?

THE RELATIONSHIP BUSINESS

"We don't repair devices, we repair relationships."

That's what my Apple (an NPS user) technician, Ciara, told me as she fixed my computer.

My little MacBook Air had been pushed to the limits and frankly so had I. I had been losing files and experiencing mail glitches for a week. I had no idea why, so I made an appointment at the Genius Bar of the closest Apple Store, two hours away.

All of these situational components could add up to a stressful experience and a grouchy customer (me!), but here's what happened instead:

1. My technician smiled as she called me by name.

2. She looked me in the eye.

3. She engaged me in conversation.

4. She demonstrated her competency without talking over my head.

5. She explained what she was doing as she did it.

6. She never made me feel bad that I couldn't solve the problem myself.

7. She told me why she works there and how much she loves her job.

Ciara was clearly a sharp and knowledgeable employee. She had a degree in computer technology and could have worked anywhere in the tech industry. When I asked her why Apple, she replied, "Because we are really in the people business. We don't repair devices, we repair relationships."

Genius.

In any business, big or small, aren't we all really in the relationship business?

Employ Ciara's techniques this week. Encourage your employees to do the same. You will diffuse grouchy. You will instill confidence. And you will gain customers for life.

Ciara did.

WHY I WAS SCARED OF MY HOTEL ROOM

If you've stayed in a hotel, you've probably seen the premium cable program guides. I found one sitting next to the TV in my hotel room in a major city. From May. In August. Some people might think an outdated pamphlet is no big deal. But, if you're like me, you may wonder, "Hmm… if they're not changing the booklet, what else are they not doing?" Like…

- Changing the sheets and pillow cases

- Wiping down the remote control

- Washing the drinking glasses

- Vacuuming the carpet

- Scrubbing the tub

- Scouring the shower

- Cleaning the coffee maker (Apparently, washing one's underwear in the coffee maker is a good thing. Google it!)

- Sanitizing door knobs

- Dusting the furniture

- Stocking clean towels

- Mopping the bathroom floor

And what exactly is IN those little bottles from the mini-bar?

Suddenly, my hotel room felt less like comfortable quarters and more like a pathogenic prison. All because of a three-month-old programming guide. In your business, do you pay attention to the small things? If you don't, your customers will.

MAPPING THE CUSTOMER EXPERIENCE

That experience at the Apple Store we mentioned earlier is no anomaly.

At an Apple Store, you don't just get the "good" employee to help you.

Apple has systems, policies, and procedures to duplicate, scale, and train on consistent customer delight.

Not only can you also do this, but you must.

Start with mapping the customer experience.

From the beginning to the end of the customer's journey, how many touchpoints can your company have with her in some fashion?

For Apple, it started with seeing their store in the mall— what it looked like and what the store decor communicated.

For you, it might be your parking lot—its cleanliness, the width of your parking spaces, funny or thoughtful signs you might have in front of the parking spaces.

How does each touchpoint make the customer feel? Does it reinforce your brand? Does it reflect Kindness and Professionalism?

Then, move on. What's your next touchpoint?

At the Apple Store, it's walking through the door to dozens of blue-shirted, bright-eyed, Apple employees. Within seconds of entry, one is sure to greet you and (noticing you carrying your laptop) intuitively inquire about service.

For you, it might be that blink-of-an-eye moment inside your front door when a customer's quick assessment of your store (or school or medical facility) raises or lowers her opinion of you.

How does the next touchpoint make the customer feel? Does it reinforce your brand? Does it reflect Kindness and Professionalism?

Map them all. Include follow-up and follow-through. Do this exercise with your whole company. You'll want everyone on board.

Take nothing for granted. Apple doesn't.

It's part of their genius. Soon, too, it will be part of yours.

HOW DO WE AVOID MISSING TOUCHPOINTS?

First, take a breath. You will, at first, miss some. It's the curse of knowledge: You've forgotten more about your business than most people will ever know.

Second, come to your senses. No, seriously—think about your customer's journey by imagining what he or she sees, hears, touches, smells, and even tastes as they work their way through your sales process and their buying processes.

Ask your team, too. What senses do we engage when a customer's doing business with us? How can we further stimulate a customer's senses when we tune these experiences?

THINK WE'RE CRAZY? RITZ-CARLTON DOESN'T, AND THEY'RE PRETTY GOOD, HUH?

Participating in a Twitter chat about customer service, someone with The Ritz-Carlton wrote:

The Ritz-Carlton ✓
@RitzCarlton

#custserv is at the core of who we are. Every stage of the guest journey provides beautiful engagement opportunities, before, during, after

← Reply ⟲ Retweeted ★ Favorited ⩘ Buffer ••• More

Hmm... "customer service is at the core of who we are."

What company doesn't say that? We bet yours does. But do you deliver? Do you over-deliver? Consistently?

Answer honestly. Now, think of the companies you know that actually do over-deliver consistently. Write them down.

Want to join them? Ritz gives you the secret in the second part of their tweet.

"Every stage of the guest journey provides beautiful engagement opportunities, before, during, after."

Okay, maybe their language is a little too rainbow-and-unicorny for you, but it still provides the key to unlocking what we call Shareworthy Customer Service systems.

Deconstruct your company's stages of the journey.

What are your company's stages?

BEFORE

From the potential customer's complete and utter unawareness of you, through the first time money changes hands:

- What are the touchpoints involved?

- What are you saying and doing that reinforces your company's values?

- What are your potential customer's friends telling her about their own experiences with your company?

- Did you deliver an experience worth talking about? In a good way?

DURING

When customer engagement is at its most visceral—from the moment they pull into your parking lot or driveway, deconstruct each interaction along the way.

How can you refine and systematize them, and fill each interaction with surprise and delight? List them.

AFTER

Here may be the greatest opportunity of all.

What are your follow-up plans to continue the conversation after someone's given you their initial business?

What can you do for your one-time customers to make them customers for life?

Break down every stage of your customer's journey, refine them, fill them with delight, and soon you, too, will be putting on the Ritz.

(UNSURPRISINGLY) RITZ-CARLTON BRINGS UP A VERY GOOD POINT ABOUT US ALL. ELMO KNOWS...

Your customer's journey involves more than just their action phase, doesn't it? If we think only about the time they're actively engaged with us, we're missing an enormous portion of the population.

We'll think about this more in the Messaging section, but the goal of advertising is to speak to each stage of a customer's journey so that your company is known, liked, and trusted BEFORE that customer reaches the ACTION stage.

What are the other stages? Elmo knows them:

THE BUYING FUNNEL

I first learned about the buying funnel more than twenty years ago from John Zimmer. After doing some research, I learned we have the late Elias St. Elmo Lewis to thank for it.

E. St. Elmo Lewis was obsessed with advertising's power to educate consumers. He recognized that not everyone was in the market for any given product or service at the same time. It was Lewis who coined the A.I.D.A. formula where first, a business must get the attention (A) of the consumer before they're able to arouse her or his interest (I). Once said interest is aroused, then and only then can a company create desire (D) in the heart of the consumer for their product or service. Once you've filled her or him with desire, you simply remove the friction to allow your now-attentive, now-interested, now-desiring customer to action (A).

Lewis' formula then migrated slightly to the above illustration.

But I believe in this Age of Rapid Distraction, with all due respect to E. St. Elmo Lewis, it's time to migrate it again.

MODERNIZING THE BUYING FUNNEL

Now that each customer is more valuable than ever, and we must strive more diligently to develop and nurture sustainable customer relationships, it's time to modify our buying funnel to reflect respect for relational customers who've placed their trust in us. We suggest a modified buying funnel that we now call The Fellowship Funnel.

Today, we need to stop thinking of a customer taking action as the end of the funnel. In truth, we are just beginning our relationship with that client.

Quick—return to your exercise in the Strategic Planning section where you calculated the lifetime value of a customer and multiplied it by four (if they recommend you to three friends who, too, stay with you for their lifetimes).

On the next page you'll see the modern buying funnel— where the sale begins the relationship:

For good fellowship with your community of customers, you must first not simply sell to them but delight them! As you think about your customer's journey, think about places you can add delight to their experience.

Once you've opened (as opposed to closed) a sale, you may now begin to befriend your customer. What ways can you connect with them, help them, offer them assistance, or educate them? How can your company be the kind of friend a friend would like to have?

As our fellowship deepens with our friends, we begin to give them extra benefits. We play favorites (more on that in a little bit). Just like frequent flyer and traveler programs, we reward loyalty with perks and privileges.

And, as a friend, you may suggest other goods and services you believe would help or delight your friend. Notice how words matter: We are no longer up-selling or cross-selling, but rather we're looking for opportunities that our friends might benefit from.

Finally, at last, we become a company in such solid fellowship with our customers that they proudly recommend us to like-minded, like-hearted friends who share their—and our—values.

But notice something: In each stage of The Fellowship Funnel, we have active, imperative verbs... UNTIL... we get to the point where it's time for referrals. That is entirely up to our customers, but because we didn't stop at the sale and because we continued to deepen our relationship with that customer, we greatly increase the likelihood of our customer introducing us to friends.

WHERE SALES RESISTANCE IS BORN

In our combined 50-plus years of doing this, we've learned sales resistance and loss of repeat and referral customers comes from one of two places:

1. When you get twitchy/pushy/aggressive and try to make people jump too far too fast in The Fellowship Funnel. Smart people and good customers are rarely convinced quickly. You want to woo your customers and build lifelong relationships with them. One-night stands rarely work out for either party.

2. You become—or revert to becoming—That Guy. Remember him? He's the guy who makes it about himself. He forgets to always—ALWAYS—put the other person's hopes and fears and wants and needs ahead of his own.

Serve, don't sell. That's how you win customers for life.

DO YOU PLAY FAVORITES WITH YOUR CUSTOMERS?

How much time and money does your company spend trying to acquire new customers?

Now, how much time and money do you spend delighting those who already do business with you?

I'm writing this while sitting in my favorite clean, well-lighted place. The owner and his family are my close friends. I know most of the managers and servers by name. I'm friends (or at least friendly) with Marijke and Dan and Elise and Art and Olivia and Annie and Isaac and Becca and Lauren and all the others.

Do I get preferential treatment here? Yes. Yes, I do. They treat me like family.

To whom do you give preferential treatment?

I ask because it occurs to me we spend an exorbitant amount of time and money to flirt and woo people who've never spent a dime with us while often turning a blind eye toward those who spend gobs of money with us over the course of their lifetimes.

Can you identify your best customers?

Have you calculated what a regular customer is worth to your business over the course of her lifetime?

How do you treat your favorite customers differently? Can we duplicate that or turn it into a system to add to our Company Constitution? Have you brainstormed ways to treat them differently?

Do you budget for treating them differently?

What's the first step toward doing this? Think over these questions and make notes of your thoughts here.

Over the 10+ years of frequenting my clean, well-lighted place, I've probably introduced more than 200 people to how amazing it is. Imagine if only half of those people started going twice a month at an average ticket of $25.

That's $50x100x12 or $60,000 a year in additional business from one preferred customer!

That's good business.

GOOD SERVICE FOR BAD CUSTOMERS

What do you do when your customers don't deserve good customer service?

Here at Tim Miles & Company, we talk about delivering Shareworthy Customer Service to your customers. It's what we firmly believe will set you apart from your competition, back up your message, and drive your social media presence.

But we probably need to talk briefly about preparing your employees to deliver Shareworthy Customer Service to EVERY customer, even the knuckleheads.

Knuckleheads by definition are rude, inappropriate, discontent, dishonest, loud, mean, or some combination of those. You know who they are. You've been behind them in line. You've flown with them. You may have even been one of them, on an isolated really-bad-day occasion.

Here are five ways to prepare your employees for the knuckleheads:

1. Teach them to expect it. People being people will have bad days. So close to the edge is our society, the slightest misalignment of service can set anyone off on any given day. Train employees to use a softer voice when confronted. To be patient. To smile. To be understanding of circumstances. Practice and role play these situations in training, so your employees will have the language to use in specific situations.

2. Give them a strong identity. What does it mean to work for your company? Make sure your employees are so keyed in on your goals and values that they know exactly how to act when confronted with a knucklehead situation. There's a great urban legend in my town, that famous actor Tom Hanks once visited a local ice cream vendor. When the young server at the window was so star-struck she couldn't speak, Hanks looked her in the eye and with great kindness and encouragement that every employer should model, said, "Amy, you can do this. You are a Custard Cup employee!" Do THAT for your employees!

3. Create a team environment. When we talked recently with managers of a Tim Horton's franchise up in Calgary, the number one thing they talked about was the importance of team. It became clear that they stood together with their

employees and they did all they could to foster a team environment.

4. Empower them to report abusive behavior. Stand behind them, and stand up for them. Better to lose a routinely unpleasant customer than a good employee. If he sees you have his back, you will have a loyal employee and a star recruiter. Your employees are your most important customers.

5. Follow up with your employees to let them know how you handled the situation. Let your employee know you have her back. Make it public with your team in your next meeting or on a poster in the break room. Let your team know—via specific examples—that you have their backs.

Knuckleheads are out there, and chances are good that we will all bump into them or even be one of them once in awhile. Get your employees ready for them so the knuckleheads won't have the power to derail your commitment to providing Shareworthy Customer Service.

TUNING YOUR CUSTOMER EXPERIENCE MAP USING YOUR CORE VALUES AND YOUR TEAM

Ready to see a practical example of improving what you measure and reward?

You've got your brand diamond. You've got your mission. Every employee knows your company's purpose.

You understand how important shared values are in today's marketplace.

Now, are you ready to take your company to the next, next, next level? Challenge your employees to come up with ideas—observable actions that reflect the values in your brand diamond.

Have a company contest. This is not a sales contest. This is for every employee in your company.

Because you share everything with your employees, they know your goals and values, so get everyone together and say:

"Each quarter for the next year, starting April 1, we're going to take 2%–5% of our quarterly customer retention budget and put it in a pot.

"As you're going through your workdays, we want you to be mindful of the entire customer experience and of the four company values that make up our brand diamond.

"Think of ways we could better demonstrate or implement our values through revised, new, or eliminated systems, policies, or procedures.

"If you submit a serious idea and a plan to implement it, you get one point. If we implement it, you get ten points. We're going to put a scoreboard in a common area, and you're each going to say what you'd do with the money.

"Then, at the end of each quarter, we'll total up the number of points and divide our money pot by that number. That gives us our bonus dollars per point. We will award each person by their earned number of points."

For example, our company's five core values are (see page 60):

1.   FAMILY

2. WISDOM

3. GENEROSITY

4. CLARITY

5. PLAYFUL

So, as we map our customer experience we would try and figure out, where could we be wiser, or more clear, or more helpful, or more playful?

Which systems, policies, and procedures should we implement to show our clients this beneficial increase in clarity or wisdom or helpfulness or playfulness?

We promise you—PROMISE YOU—this will be the best share of your marketing budget you spend the rest of this year. Unless, of course, you also do this...

TUNING THE CUSTOMER EXPERIENCE

Want to be more like Disney, Apple, and the Ritz? You've already started by mapping your customer experience.

Now, how can you baseline, improve, and systematize the experiences at each of those touchpoints?

You MUST do this as a company, not have it dictated from top-down ownership. You need your company to own these ideas together.

Start Tuning with Your Brand Diamond

Remember your brand diamond: the four (or so) values that reflect how your company thinks, acts, and sees the world?

Your brand diamond includes values that should embody your company's non-negotiable standards. They are the lens through which you evaluate potential new hires, establish new company policies, and determine how you delight your customers.

Once you have your brand diamond, take the customer experience map that you've created, and brainstorm ways to use the values on your brand diamond at each touchpoint. Adjust each customer touchpoint using these values.

Similars

Remember when you identified companies similar to yours when uncovering your company's true core values? Take another look at those companies outside your industry. What systems, policies, and procedures do they use that reinforce those values? As a group, discover whether you can adapt them to delight your own customers.

CONTINUE OPTIMIZING USING THE 14 FACETS

Figure out ways to improve each experience along the way using the same techniques used by Apple, Disney, and Nordstrom (they employ the 14 facets—even if they don't call them that).

Ask:

"HOW COULD WE MAKE A CUSTOMER'S EXPERIENCE AT TOUCHPOINT A MORE PLAYFUL (ONE OF THE FOURTEEN)?"

... and ...

"How could we leverage privilege (another of the fourteen) to enrich customers' experiences at Touchpoint C?"

Work through the list of fourteen as a team. It'll be a paradigm-shifting experience, we promise you.

We're building consistent systems that can be scaled and bound, to easily train new employees.

It is a bit like spreadsheet-work, but it ensures you'll be able to consciously decide how customers are treated at every step along their path with you.

"JUST PAYING ATTENTION..."

"Well hello, Tim!" she said, as if we were old friends— only we weren't old friends or even friends. She was my restaurant server the day before... and I had never given her my name.

Chrystal would be my server this day as well, and before I sat down, she was pouring my coffee. As she poured, she said:

"Coffee again today, Tim? And water, too?"

"Umm, yes. Yes! Please..." I said, still trying to figure out how she knew my name.

At this point, I should mention that I had been staying at the delightful Hotel Blackfoot in Calgary. It's a busy hotel and hotel restaurant. I say this because Chrystal very likely had dozens of other tables and customers the day of my first visit. So, my surprise (and delight) continued when she came to take my order and said:

"Same as yesterday, Tim, or would you like to try something new?"

"Oh, I think same as yesterday, thank you... I'll have—," I said.

"Pancakes, yes, and brown toast, right?" she said.

"Umm, yes. Yes! Please..." I said, *still* trying to figure out how she knew my name.

I had to know her secret. "Chrystal," I said, at the end of breakfast, "what's your secret?"

"Soory?" she asked. (I'm still unsure how to spell the Canadian version of "sorry" but it sounds way cooler than the American version.)

"You knew my name when I came in," I said.

"Oh that," she said, downplaying it, "I just remembered it off the ticket you signed."

"Okay," I said, still impressed, "so how did you remember my order amidst all the other customers, whose orders I'm assuming you remembered, too. What's your secret?"

"Just paying attention."

How well do your employees pay attention? How well do they focus, even if it's just for perhaps three seconds at a clip? How do you expect me to ever pick another Calgary hotel or restaurant when I visit Canada? Or how can you expect me to recommend another hotel or restaurant to my friends and colleagues (including you)?

Yes, your regular customers deserve preferential treatment, but it's worth mapping your customer experience for new customers as well. It's worth asking yourself as you fine-tune your touchpoints how simple, free tools like kindness, focus, and memory can help you turn a simple encounter into an unforgettable one.

IN THE WORKBOOK VERSION OF BRAND YOUR OWN BUSINESS, WE PROVIDE 12 PAGES OF EXERCISES TO HELP YOU AND YOUR TEAM MAP AND TUNE YOUR CUSTOMER EXPERIENCE.

TO ORDER OR LEARN MORE ABOUT THE BYOB WORKBOOK, VISIT:

BRANDYOUROWN.BUSINESS

INTERMISSION

Want some good news? The hard work is done. If you've put real effort into the simple-but-not-easy chapters and exercises you've already completed, the rest is child's play.

Want even better news? There are thousands of advertising companies ready, willing, and able to take your money for these last two sections, and our experience has shown us that you don't need them unless you simply don't have the time to work on messaging and media yourself.

If that's the case, before we're done, we'll give you a method for evaluating companies you might like to hire. We'll help you separate partners from predators. Before we continue though, here's a question to which we legitimately have no certain answer but two good guesses:

Why are there thousands of companies and maybe millions of books, white papers, videos, and blog posts devoted to these top two tiers of The First Order Of Business, but virtually none devoted to building a solid foundation that makes developing the top two so much simpler? Our guesses:

1. The top two are fun. You get to play with toys and consider yourself "creative" if you work in and with the top two tiers. It's also very high margin to work with the top two with Fortune 500 companies and obscenely well funded startups.

2. The top two require little oversight. If you haven't spent time working on the foundation, ad agencies and media professionals can simply point you toward their favorite tools and tricks (and the

ones they receive the highest commission for) because you don't know better.

Well, now that you've studied the importance and understand the elegance of the first three tiers, you know better, don't you?

AS MY DAUGHTER WOULD SAY, "YOU ARE A BIG OL' BUCKET OF CRAZY AWESOME! HAVE A DOUGHNUT!"

Quality content means content that is packed with clear utility and is brimming with inspiration, and it has relentless empathy for the audience...

ANN HANDLEY

January 2014

SECTION FOUR

MESSAGING

DOES CREATIVITY STILL MATTER?

Not that long ago, clever was enough. If you had enough cash and hired a creative enough team to produce your marketing campaign, you'd assure your company some degree of success.

Those days went the way of the Dodo Bird and 8-track tapes.

Does clever still matter? Absolutely, it's just that it's everywhere... including always at our fingertips.

Check your Facebook or Twitter feed... or just wait for someone to text you the latest clever thing. There are a bazillion clever things being created every day.

How do you make sure your message is heard, seen, and remembered?

Creativity. In fact, creativity's more important than ever! Sounds like something of a paradox, doesn't it? Welcome to advertising in the 21st century!

Here's where creativity comes in: In messaging, relevance doesn't mean boring—you can use creativity to come up with strange, *captivating* ways to arouse interest BUT you have to quickly—like, speed of light quickly—bridge back to whatever benefit is in it for the customer. Or you've lost them just as sure as if you'd been boring with your messaging.

And you've got to be clear—crystal clear—about how your product or service benefits potential customers in your messaging.

MESSAGING VS. COPY

Which came first?

The chicken or the egg?

The question or the answer?

Orange the color or orange the fruit?

Messaging or copy? "Wait a minute. Aren't messaging and copy the same thing?"

Well...they're related, yes, but copy and messaging are NOT the same.

Messaging is determining WHAT you will talk about.

Copy is determining HOW you will say it.

You have to be good at messaging before you can excel at copywriting.

As you follow The First Order of Business, you develop systems, policies, procedures, hiring practices, etc. that help you determine how you will delight your customers. Once you know where you want to go, how you'll get there, and what you stand for, then you can begin developing your own unique brand of messaging.

While crafting your message, answer these three questions:

1. Is your message relevant?

Remember Ivan Pavlov? Every day, ol' Ivan would rub meat paste on his dog's tongue and ring a bell. Eventually, he could simply make his dog salivate with the sound of that bell. Now, if Mr. Pavlov had kicked his dog square in the kibbles and bits every time he rang the bell, the response would have been dramatically different. Pavlov's experiment succeeded because, well, dogs love the taste of meat. Otherwise, the incessant ringing of the bell would have done nothing more than irritate the poop out of the dog. What is the meat your customers crave? A message has relevance to the degree it speaks to that craving in the heart of your customer.

2. Does your message have credibility?

Simply stated, a message has credibility if it's believable. Can you substantiate the claims in your messaging? Will you keep the promises you make to your customers? Can you identify and address the loopholes in your messaging before your prospect has a chance to become skeptical?

3. Is your message authentic?

Are you who you say you are? Is the message a true reflection of your goals and values? Customers are invited to your place of business to see the real you every day. This means you must deliver what you say you stand for.

Feeble messaging is weak because it's not connected to your company's core values, or it talks about stuff your customers don't care about.

Figure out the WHAT before attempting the HOW.

THE KEY TO MAXIMUM CREATIVITY? A SPREADSHEET! (WHAT IS A MESSAGE CALENDAR AND WHY DO YOU NEED ONE?)

Have advertising due dates ever snuck up on you? You committed to some advertising and then... well, kinda forgot about what to say in that advertising. A message calendar makes it much simpler to always be prepared to either create messaging yourself or hand off the right information to whomever creates your ads. By giving forethought to messaging and copy, you're sure to have more effective, more powerful advertising and marketing.

Well, almost always—we tell our clients that a message calendar will ensure that at least 80% of our entire year will be proactive when it comes to knowing what to say in every media channel we select. Usually, it turns out to be more like 95%, but we never know what surprises may pop up.

There are three elements to a message calendar, and they fit nicely into a simple spreadsheet

1. TIME-FRAMES/HOLIDAYS

First of all, consider how your business breaks up a year. The default breakdown is monthly, but that doesn't necessarily reflect your business category. For example, heating and air conditioning companies don't necessarily break up their year by months (12) but rather by seasons (4). Don't be tethered to the calendar months. If you know, for example, that you have a busy season that runs from Groundhog Day to Arbor Day, break out your calendar accordingly. We have one retail client who breaks down their year into thirteen four-week "windows." List these time-frames in column A of your spreadsheet. Additionally, you might want to note important holidays on the message calendar to create a special—if short-term—theme.

2. THEMES

Next, you'll need a core message or primary topic for each time-frame. Maybe you're going to promote a specific collection of furniture or talk about cruise season. For heating and air conditioning companies in the southern United States, they pretty much know it's going to be hot in the summer. That doesn't sneak up on them. It shouldn't sneak up on you, either.

One thing you'll notice is that it's very likely your message calendar will be very similar from one year to the next. That's not a bad thing. In fact, it's a very good thing. Groups of consumers are as comfortably predictable as the seasons of your business. Your theme or themes—no more than three per period—go in column B. If you have more than one primary theme, make sure you have enough touchpoints and media channels to give each theme the attention it deserves. For most family businesses, we recommend no more than a primary theme and secondary theme.

3. TOUCHPOINTS/MEDIA CHANNELS

The remaining columns of your spreadsheet will comprise the different media channels or touchpoints you'll use to share your theme(s) with the public. These may include (but not be limited to) a radio campaign, window displays, in-store signage and other collateral material, content marketing, social media, employee promotions/contests, etc.

And while your first two columns should remain somewhat untouched once you've created them, these remaining media and touchpoint columns might be somewhat fluid as you add or remove channels or touchpoints. The important thing at the genesis of your message calendar is that you and your team give willful thought to how each theme might be best represented by the channels and touchpoints you currently use.

Then, about a month before each new timeframe approaches, review your message calendar, your themes, and your touchpoints to make sure you're prepared. Yes, put this in your own day-planner or calendar no less than one month before the next timeframe. With your message calendar, there's no excuse for not being prepared for 80–95% of the messaging your company will need throughout the year, and when you're prepared, your messaging is sure to be more effective and efficient.

The first pass at a message calendar should take no more than half a day, and those few hours will pay dividends for years to come.

MORE ADS! MORE OFTEN!

The reason we're spending so much time thinking about messaging and creating a message calendar is because our attention spans have shrunk to the size of urinal gnats.

Once we're committed to our values, and we've got a Company Constitution filled with reasons to do business with us, we need more ads more often.

They need a consistent focus, but they need to capture the attention of your audience and build equity with them like bricks in a wall.

If you're creating more ads, you're going to need a guide to help you write more effectively and efficiently. So... here...

THE NEW A.I.D.A.: UPDATING THE FORMULA FOR COPYWRITING TO R.A.C.E.S. & C.A.R.S.

Attention, Interest, Desire, Action (A.I.D.A.)... in 1898, the aforementioned Elias St. Elmo Lewis provided copywriters with a four-step formula for developing advertising.

1. **ATTRACT ATTENTION**
2. **MAINTAIN INTEREST**
3. **CREATE DESIRE**
4. **MOVE TO ACTION**

And while you might argue—and we might not disagree with you—that advertising formulas run the danger of producing predictable, formulaic advertising, how can you argue that, for more than a century, Lewis' formula has helped more professionals market more goods and services that any other process?

It's time for a change.

We've hurtled headlong into an era of rapid distraction. Our attention muscles have atrophied, and we're more skeptical than ever. Recently our team articulated a new process to get to the point and back it up more quickly.

1. **RELEVANCE**

2. **AUTHENTICITY**

3. **CAPTIVATING**

4. **ELEPHANT**

5. **STORIES**

6. **CREDIBILITY**

7. **ACTION**

8. **RELEVANCE**

9. **SOCIAL PROOF**

The R.A.C.E.S. & C.A.R.S. process works for ads, landing pages, sales videos, and more. While not altogether sequential, it provides a perfect checklist for reviewing your message.

Unless you're talking to me about what matters to me **(RELEVANCE)** right out of the gate, you've lost me because there are way too many distractions in my world. You have to immediately open with: why and how does this affect the consumer?

When talking with consumers, it's equally critical—as we've discussed—to talk in the language of your customer (as opposed to your own technical terminology or in a language of clichés and brochure-speak) and letting them see the real you **(AUTHENTICITY)**.

As you read in the introduction to this section, you're fighting for attention, and we don't believe creativity is the right "c" word. We believe it's **CAPTIVATING**. How can we get you to stop thinking about what's on your mind and switch to our message?

We're increasingly skeptical, so how can we anticipate and overcome the **ELEPHANT**s in the room? What are the "yeah, buts..." potential customers give you? How do you overcome them? Your message developer needs to be regularly updated on all the "yeah, buts..."

Why did Jesus speak so often in parables? In Matthew 13:10-13 (NKJV), he explains when asked:

> *And the disciples came and said to Him, "Why do You speak to them in parables?"*
>
> *He answered and said to them, "Because it has been given to you to know the mysteries of the kingdom of heaven, but to them it has not been given. For whoever has, to him more will be given, and he will have abundance; but whoever does not have, even what he has will be taken away from him. Therefore I speak to them in parables, because seeing they do not see, and hearing they do not hear, nor do they understand."*

We connect to each other through the symbolic language of **STORIES**. Too often, we've witnessed business owners attempt to communicate in grand, sweeping statements, but we don't live our lives in grand, sweeping statements. We live our lives and connect to one another through small stories of little moments. It's what made the show *Seinfeld* so successful. They claimed the show was about nothing; it was about those little stories that connect us. For more on this subject, we, once again, refer you to *Buyer Legends* by the Eisenbergs.

Stories increase **CREDIBILITY**! When you ask an employee, "Can you tell me a story from the last week where you got to use [Core Value]?" You'll see her eyes light up, and she'll tell you a story that shows you walk the talk of that value. Hearkening back to ELEPHANT, you'll also want to be sure and cite your sources for statistics and quotes. If you simply say, "4 out of 5 doctors recommend us..." We'll assume those four doctors are either your friends or in your pocket.

Now that you've worked so hard to persuade someone, we want to make it as simple as possible for them to take **ACTION**. Once they have the confidence they need to do whatever it is you want them to do next, how do they do it? Make sure you're clear as polished glass.

Then you've come full circle **(RELEVANCE)**... back to a potential customer imagining herself as having benefited from doing business with you...

Finally, we want to know who else has benefited from this **(SOCIAL PROOF)**? Give testimonials or reviews from people just like me whose problem—my problem—you've solved.

THE BEST WAY TO GET GREAT SOCIAL PROOF

If you deliver a great product and experience to your customers, you should have no trouble getting them to say so, but over the years, we've learned there are several techniques that work better to save you (and them) time and get the best quotes bragging about your business (remember, you never want to be the one bragging about your business). As you'll recall from the introductory section, you don't want to be That Guy.

NET PROMOTER SCORE VERBATIMS

Remember how we recommend measuring Shareworthy Customer Service with the world's shortest survey? Remember the second question where you ask customers the number one reason for their score? These can provide you with a wealth of valuable, actual responses from customers. With their permission, you can use these on in-store signage, collateral material, social media, your website, and many other places.

INTERVIEWS

Oftentimes, customers will be happy to conduct a short interview with you about their experience of doing business with your company. These may be conducted in person or over the phone or some sort of computer video conference. Once again, with permission, you may record and use these in your advertising. Authentic, unscripted video and audio are powerful tools vouching for you. Here are some questions we recommend asking (and we also recommend you ask your interview subject to begin their answer by restating your question).

"What was the problem or initial incident that caused you to come see us/use us/call us?"

"Was there anything in particular that made you choose us over other companies?"

"Can you just briefly walk me through your experience with us?"

"Would you recommend us to a friend? What's the number one reason you'd recommend us to a friend?"

"Anything else you'd like people to know about us?"

"HAPPY CHECKS"

These are similar to the interviews above but less formal; however, one big distinction is that they're made by the business owner specifically. There's a tremendous amount of equity in being asked your opinion and feedback by the business owner him or herself. As the owner, make a point to do two or three of these calls (or more if time permits) each day. Not only will you gather some insightful feedback and great social proof, but it's some of the best marketing you can do to let customers know the owner cares about their experiences.

WHEN YOU DON'T KNOW WHAT TO SAY

"I never know what to say in my commercials."

"What information should I feature on my website?"

"We don't do Facebook or Twitter because we don't know what to post."

"A newsletter? What am I going to say in a newsletter?"

You can solve this challenge in three simple steps:

1.   Ask each of your employees to write down the top three most-asked questions from your customers.

2.   Compile a master list of questions.

3.   Go through the list and write an answer to every question.

There. Now you know what to say.

Ask your employees to constantly keep a running list of new questions. This will keep you well-stocked with topics to write about. This can evolve into a delightful F.A.Q. section on your website, and if you have someone on your staff comfortable with technology, you can even shoot videos answering each one of the questions so we get to know you a little. Even if you shoot the videos, be sure to include a transcription of the video. Some people prefer to read rather than watch, and Google can't hear your video, but it can read your text, and you will be rewarded for your relevant, user-friendly content via its organic and local search rankings.

PINBALL MARKETING

I love pinball. I hate multi-ball. In case you've never (shame on you) played pinball, multi-ball is the dreaded moment during the game when multiple balls are unlocked and launched into play.

Multi-ball frustrates the bejeebus out of me.

When I'm playing with one ball, I can give 100% of my time, effort, and attention to that shiny silver orb. But when other balls start entering the fray, I lose my cool, my focus, and the game (in that order).

Unfortunately, a lot of the advertising you see and hear is like multi-ball.

Think of the pinball as the one main idea that you want to drive home in your marketing. Instead of making it easy for your potential customer to focus on what you want them to know, advertisers throw a bunch of other balls into the mix and cram as much information as they can into their ad. Just watch or listen to any commercial and you'll probably hear:

But wait, there's more... (ball!)

And that's not all... (ball!)

Plus... (ball!)

What's more... (ball!)

Be sure to ask about our... (ball!)

And don't forget... (ball!)

Multi-ball.

Do you want your ads to fly past the flippers in your customer's already crowded mind? Stop lobbing balls at them. If you have seven different ideas to promote about your business, don't jam all seven into one overstuffed, inefficient message. Instead, commit to a campaign of seven different marketing messages with each message focusing on one of the ideas. This concept isn't limited to radio and TV commercials, either. Focus on one idea for every:

- Print Ad
- Blog Post

- Social Media Update

- Billboard

- Web Page

- Banner Ad

- Poster

- Article

- Brochure

- Email Newsletter

- YouTube Video

- Sign

- Coupon

- Direct Mail Piece

- Bus Board

- Text Message

- Vehicle Wrap

- Flyer

- Door Hanger

- Yard Sign

- Promotional Item

- Airplane Banner

One Ball = One Idea

Multi-ball = Bad Idea

Don't think "Ad"—Think "Campaign."

ADS, GIVEN THE PROPER REPETITIOUS ELEMENTS, CAN BUILD EQUITY. THE WHOLE CAN BECOME GREATER THAN THE SUM OF ITS PARTS.

Most companies have started a great campaign only to drop it too quickly, before it had a chance to begin to really compound its value.

We know, for example, that when we hear that fiddle music and Tom Bodett's voice, that Motel 6 has clean, comfortable rooms for the lowest price of any national chain. We don't know what else he might say or where he might lead us, but we know him, and we know Motel 6.

They've built a style guide for their hotels through writing and voice and music and pace.

Companies often tell us they think they need a jingle.

We get what they're saying, which is really:

> *"We need some sort of signature that we can use in all our ads."*

Melody and meter help. They sneak in through the side door of the brain. It's why you know all those songs you never intended to learn. Sound is powerful.

But most jingles are poorly written. Companies that want jingles have the right idea, though. Look for things you can repeat in each ad. Give us some signature ingredients we know we can expect. The rest? Keep us surprised, please.

ASTERISKS

Asterisks suggest you're not telling me the whole story.

Asterisks suggest restrictions may apply.

Asterisks suggest your free offer's gonna cost me a bundle.

Asterisks suggest I'm gonna be jumping through hoops.

Asterisks suggest you're gonna talk me into something I don't want.

Asterisks suggest you're keeping a secret.

Asterisks suggest I'm going to pay more in the long run.

Asterisks suggest that something shady is afoot.

Asterisks suggest a lot of legal-eagle, red-tape, mumbo-jumbo gobbledygook.

Asterisks suggest you're trying to pull a fast one.

Do you want your clients to believe you?

Do you want your patrons to trust you?

Do you want customers to buy from you?

Lose the asterisks.

THE MORTAL SIN OF MESSAGING: CLICHÉS

Turn on a radio. Watch local television. Open a newspaper. Drive by a billboard. Read through a website.

Now count the clichés.

Identifying a cliché is simple. Just listen for the most overused, overworked, hackneyed, predictable, unoriginal, uninspired collection of crummy copywriting. You'll know it when you hear it.

That is, if you hear it at all. Therein lies the danger of a cliché. The more a tired slogan is used, the less it's actually heard. And the less effective it becomes.

Clichés cause us to tune out.

So, why the heck do we still use them?

Reason #1: They're EASY

You're a copywriter. You've spent all day writing ad after ad. You're tired. Your brain is mush.

Or you're rushed. The deadline is looming. You have to write something and you have to write it NOW.

You could carefully craft a painstakingly persuasive message that cuts through the clutter and truly speaks to the heart of the consumer.

Or you could simply throw together some crappy clichés and be on your way.

Reason #2: You don't have anything else to say

It's hard to write an ad for a business if the business owner doesn't give you anything remarkable to say.

Clichés fill the void left by lack of good information.

And they must be stopped.

So...

As a service to the business community, here are the six most obnoxious, abhorrent, offensive, despicable, and overused clichés in advertising.

Full disclosure: I've used them all. I'm not proud. I was young and I needed the money.

DIFFERENT

Last week, we received an email from the owner of an heating and air company we work with, expressing concern about the radio stations on which his ads were about to start airing.

His concern wasn't so much about the radio stations, per se, but about his competitors' ads that already air on those stations.

To his discerning ear, the other heating and air companies' ads sounded very similar to each other in their production, style, concept, and delivery. He feared that the ads that we produced for his company wouldn't be as effective because they didn't have quite the same sound as all the competition.

His email immediately caused me to flash back to 1998.

At the time, Ryan and I slaved away as lowly production people at a cluster of small market radio stations. We had been tasked with creating a radio ad for a local motorcycle dealership. We knew that other bike dealers were crowding the airwaves with the usual clichés such as gimmicky sales, special financing rates, and rebates.

We chose a different route.

Instead of shouting about prices, discounts, or zero percent financing, Ryan and I produced the audio equivalent of a test drive. We put the listener on the bike. Our hope was that our commercial would cause the listener to visualize the open road, hear the rumble of the bike, and feel the wind in his hair.

It was unlike anything else on the air. We were mighty proud of that ad. We couldn't wait to present it to the client.

When we finished playing the commercial, there was a long pause on the other end of the phone line. The owner of the dealership then said 11 words that knocked me on my butt:

"Can't you just make a commercial that sounds like everyone else?"

No joke. That's what he said.

And that's exactly what we did.

By the way, he's not in business anymore.

We get it. Being different is risky. It's scary. It makes you vulnerable to ridicule and criticism, but it can also be a powerful weapon in your marketing arsenal.

I'm not saying you should be different for the sake of being different. That's not advertising. That's annoying, but if you have a strong, personal, unique message built on your goals and values, strategic planning, and customer experience, it's okay to say it in a different, more believable, unpolished, persuasive way.

Sure, it's easy and safe to blend in with the crowd. But when you look and sound like everyone else, don't be shocked when nobody finds you.

"NO LOGO OR NOTHIN'?"

"Are you sure you sent us the right thing?"

One of my clients had purchased ad space in a restaurant's menu. We had just delivered it when the restaurant called us back. After a moment of panic and double-checking, we confirmed that yes, we had sent them the right thing.

"We've just never seen anything like this before. Are you sure you want to run this?"

"Yes."

"But there's no logo or nothin'."

"Yes."

"It doesn't look like any of the other ads!"

"Yes."

Why is it that so many people believe ads should look, sound, and read like ads? Isn't the point to NOT make it look like everyone else's?

"The real truth is," said Howard Luck Gossage, "no one reads an ad. People read what interests them. Sometimes it's an ad."

This restaurant is a popular location for blue-collar folks to frequent in our client's trade area. We can promise you not one of them wants to read an ad—in spite of the fact that several thousand each month get a menu handed to them. All we had to do was give them something interesting to read. How about you? Do your ads look, sound and feel like ads?

For a good time*, call 988-8688

*and not just a good time, but a good career and a great place to work where we pay higher than what's average for heating and air conditioning companies. Now, we're picky ... understand we expect a lot of you, and we expect you to expect a lot out of us, too. Hope you could follow that there. Here at Pass One Hour Heating & Air, we are always looking for honest, mannerly people who are looking to go from good to great and be part of something special. HVAC experience a big, big, big plus. Manners and responsibility mandatory. We are growing, and if you're a good person with good skills, we need you!

---

10 BASIC STEPS TO AD WRITING

1. If it's a new product category or business, or you're unfamiliar with it, do some keyword/trigger and consumer research.

2. What's the goal of your ad? Are you promoting an event or trying to build a brand?

3. Are you speaking to relational or transactional customers? To dig more deeply, which one of your personas are you speaking to?

4. Know your one main idea. See it clearly. Is it to position yourself against a competitor? Is it to build credibility?

5. Know the ad's one key takeaway. Have more than one? Then you have more than one ad to write.

6. Know your brand diamond and your company's why. Make sure your ad properly filters through these.

7. Know how you want to end. What do you want the consumer to do next?

8. Anticipate any objections. Address them. This may require an ad campaign.

9. What mood do you want to convey? Choose music to put you in that mind frame—this isn't music for the ad, this is tonal music to help you write the ad.

10. Eliminate all other distractions. Close email and turn off your phone.

11. Pick a voice. Who's the narrator of your story? The business owner? A customer? John Cusack? Who?

12. Open big. Serve up a juicy first mental image in the headline, opening shot, or opening line.

13. Bridge to the benefit your business delivers, but show the benefit. Don't tell her you're courteous. Open her door.

14. Write a long, crappy first draft.

15. Find any claims you make. Substantiate them. Prove it.

16.   Kill any clichés and ad speak.

17.   Whack adjectives. Amplify your verbs.

18.   Make sure you're talking about the customer more than yourself.

19.   Be active. Put the customer in the scene of your ad.

20.   Edit it for clarity.

21.   Proofread it. Have someone else proof it, too.

22.   Edit it again for clarity.

23.   Perform the ad for five people and ask them two questions:

       1. What was the main idea?

       2. Does this accurately reflect our company values?

If at least four of the five don't give you the same answer to the first question in Step #23 and all five don't respond "yes" to the second question, please return to Step #1. Lather. Rinse. Repeat.

There you go. Sorry, there aren't just ten steps, and it isn't basic.

IN THE WORKBOOK VERSION OF BRAND YOUR OWN BUSINESS, WE PROVIDE 13 ADDITIONAL LESSONS AND 8 PAGES OF EXERCISES TO HELP YOU AND YOUR TEAM MAKE YOUR MESSAGE MORE POWERFUL.

TO ORDER OR LEARN MORE ABOUT THE BYOB WORKBOOK, VISIT:

BrandYourOwn.Business

"I hate writing. I love having written."

-Dorothy Parker

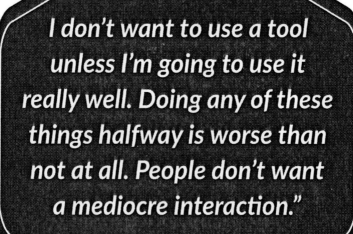

I don't want to use a tool unless I'm going to use it really well. Doing any of these things halfway is worse than not at all. People don't want a mediocre interaction."

SETH GODIN

February
2008

SECTION FIVE

MEDIA

WOULD YOU LIKE TO ENSURE THE HIGHEST AND BEST USE OF YOR MONEY?

Sure, media choices and placement matter. You can waste a metric ton of money if you're not careful.

Make sure the other four foundations of The First Order of Business are sound and solid.

We've never seen a business fail because they reached the wrong people, but sadly, we've seen too many fail for saying the wrong thing, saying nothing at all, or delivering a poor experience.

Once you're following The First Order of Business, we believe less is more when it comes to media.

So, which media do you choose, and how do you legitimately become a player in each one, and are you putting enough time, money, energy, and talent into all three types?

Wait... you knew there were three, didn't you? Don't worry if you didn't. We'll get to that as well as several other principles that will make you much more confident to make decisions about budgeting for and choosing media channels in the weeks, months, and even years to come.

That's actually a pretty bold statement... whether you know it yet or not. Why? Nothing in marketing is changing more rapidly than this top tier of our pyramid.

WHY IT'S HARD TO WRITE ABOUT MEDIA IN A BOOK TODAY

Whenever possible, I like to write in specifics, as they're far more helpful and believable than generalities, but between now (when I'm typing this) and when you're reading this, we can't possibly estimate how many changes there will be to the media landscape.

For example, my colleagues and I are experimenting with advertising on Pandora in select markets around the US. In early 2017, in nine out of ten major U.S. markets where we've bought enough Pandora advertising to make a dent, we've been extremely disappointed with the results.

But, also in early 2017 as I write this, Pandora is still very much making up its advertising rules as it goes along. That may not be true when you read this. Heck, Pandora may be gone by the time you read this. Like so many critical darlings, it's not exactly wildly profitable, nor may it ever be.

Another example? Terrestrial radio. Not a week goes by where I don't read an article that doesn't even include terrestrial radio as a current, viable media channel for message distribution among paid media.

Yet, I can tell you that our clients buy approximately USD$10,000,000 in radio, and all of them run 52 weeks a year because it reaches millions of people more effectively and more emotionally than any other medium we can purchase for our clients' dollars.

Does that mean mass media isn't losing its mass? On the contrary, just as Yellow Pages, Magazine, and Newspaper audiences shrank, I expect the same to happen to "old media" like broadcast television, cable television, and radio.

They just haven't yet. In early 2017, they're still working very, very well for us, and it makes me smile when I read of their dismissal by young tech upstart thought leaders. I don't get frustrated. I give thanks. That's less noise, clutter, and competition for our wildly successful clients.

But don't think we're not thinking long and hard about what to do when terrestrial radio eventually becomes a less viable option.

Our company's paid by how much our clients grow... not by how much or where they spend their advertising dollars. It's important for us to constantly read, study, and experiment (with our own company's money) on what's working, what isn't, and why.

Now, when Google and Elon Musk and the other auto companies perfect autonomous vehicles, please ask me again how I feel about radio.

ABOUT THE MEDIA SECTION OF THIS BOOK

We're going to give you as many practical, timeless principles as we can to help you make decisions about how much to invest and how to think about the virtually infinite choices that face business owners today.

Last generation, it was much easier if for no other reason than a profoundly smaller number of media channels. But today? You're faced with questions about not only new channels but new channels you don't understand. Yet, there are experts—and reams and reams of virtual paper—professing why you should choose each of those media.

Pinterest? It's the best!

Facebook? It's the best!

Retargeting? It's the best!

Ads on DogsThatLookLikeKennyRogers.com? The best!

There are an awful lot of so-called experts completely dismissing every media channel your business considered just a few years ago.

What I want to provide for you in this section is a framework for making decisions, for a general evaluation of your advertising budget, and a way to select someone to help you navigate the rapidly changing media landscape if you so choose.

THE FIRST—AND FROG-SWALLOWING AWFULLEST—THING YOU'VE GOTTA DO

You're going to have to audit how, where, and how much you're marketing. Here's the best way to do it.

STEP #1: Make an exhaustive list of every marketing activity your company engages in. Gather the troops via email or in your virtual office or in your bricks and mortar building and work together to create an exhaustive list. Remember not only paid advertising but anything you do that promotes your company or brand.

STEP #2: Let it sit. Review the list in a couple of days. Run it by the group. Add anything you may have missed.

STEP #3: Host a sorting session via virtual or actual office with your team. These four questions will help you sort your marketing activity into useful buckets:

What's right? What's working well? What accurately reflects our values?

What's wrong? What's broken and not serving our staff or customers?

What's missing? What should we be doing in marketing that we are not?

What's confusing? What are we doing that is unclear in our message?

STEP #4: Once your lists are made, have four conversations:

How can we amplify what's right? Talk through each item and list out potential improvements.

How can we change what's wrong? Examine each item and decide how to correct.

How can we add what's missing? Discuss missing items and identify how to add them.

Refine the murky items for clarity.

STEP #5: Take your four lists and create actions items. Each action item should include:

Action Steps: What needs to be done?

Responsible Party: Who is ultimately responsible to make sure it gets done? A team may work on it, but you want one person accountable for each action step.

Due Date: When is it expected to be done?

Support Source: Where will the responsible party turn for help?

If you tackle one of these steps and sub-steps at your weekly staff meetings in first quarter, by the start of second quarter, you will have an amazing action plan for marketing that will transform your company or organization for the better.

THE FALSE-CONSENSUS EFFECT

"Well, we don't even want to try Pandora. I'm sure everybody who listens pays for Pandora One, which eliminates all the ads."

What makes you say that?

"Well, it's only $36 a year to get rid of all the ads. I'm sure everyone thinks that's worth it."

Wait... do you have Pandora One?

"Of course! And I'm sure everyone else does, too."

If you've ever assumed everyone else thinks the way you do, congratulations, you've fallen under the spell of the False-Consensus Effect.

At one time or another we've all believed everyone feels the same way we do or makes the same decisions we would.

WAIT—see what I just did there? I fell under its spell, too.

I include it here to simply say that analytics are your friend, if only to remind you that not everyone thinks, acts, and sees the world the same way as you do.

And while losing some of their mass slowly and steadily, your local TV news still gets watched by thousands, tens of thousands, or possibly millions depending on your market size. And that radio station you loathe? It's still heard by metric crap-tons of people, too.

That's important to remember.

HOW MANY NEW CUSTOMERS DO YOU NEED?

Let's say you have only enough money to buy a small radio station in a medium-sized market with a metro population of, say, 600,000.

Let's say their number of weekly listeners is a paltry 10,000. I mean, they clunk there on the bottom in some weird little electronic polka format that nobody likes, right?

Well, no, it's not nobody.

Please show me one business who doesn't want 10,000 new customers, and because of comparative analytics and economics, I'm going to be able to own those 10,000 potential customers with more frequency than I could afford with stations with more listeners.

It's easy to get lost inside the numbers of mass media. It's easy to get discouraged by low analytics numbers on your website or email marketing or Facebook campaign.

I'm telling you right now to look past those numbers and focus on one number as it relates to any raw number of listeners, viewers, openers, clickers, or unique monthly visitors.

LAST-CLICK ATTRIBUTION ABSOLUTION

Another media slippery slope is something called *last-click attribution*. As its name suggests, last-click attribution's a fallacy through which we give credit—sole credit—to whatever media channel brought a customer into contact with us.

For example, let's say you have an email subscriber who clicked on a coupon in your most recent email. That customer clicks through to your website, adds the item to a shopping cart, and purchases the item.

That customer's value can be directly tied to that email, correct?

Well, yes... and no... how about another example?

Your television ad campaign has a unique phone number at the end. If someone calls that number (which you track using a third-party vendor), they must have seen your television ad and decided they needed your product or service, correct?

Definitely... maybe...

We rarely make decisions in a vacuum.

In the first example, that customer ended up on your email list thanks to a different message/campaign, right? And they must've had a good customer experience in prior shopping trips (both off and online), right? Do those previous interactions affect this current decision to purchase? Of course they do.

In the second example, how many times had the customer seen your TV ad before this viewing? What kind of opinion had this customer formed of your company before his need arose? Is it possible the customer checked online or with friends about your reputation before they called that number? And what if that customer was moved to act by your ad but couldn't remember the phone number? What if, instead, he saw the ad but then got your number from his phone?

To what should we attribute this customer's decision to purchase?

All of it!

It's easy to fall into the trap of last-click attribution, but you should keep in mind it isn't easy, and it's rarely singular. Sorry.

But you're forgiven... just like the False Consensus Effect, it's an easy—and convenient—mistake to make.

HOW, THEN, DO YOU MEASURE RESPONSE?

If you would like to begin accurately measuring:

1. Your repeat and referral customers

2. Your location-driven customers

3. Your advertising-driven customers

Here's how it's done:

First, EVERY customer who enters the store needs to be counted so that you have a total count to serve as a baseline for your percentages.

EVERY customer who enters the store needs to be asked, "Is this your first visit?"

If "No," they are obviously a repeat customer. Smile broadly and say, "Welcome back!"

If "Yes," then ask, "Did you hear about us from a friend, or through our advertising, or did you just see the store and decide to pop in?"

Note: NEVER ASK, "How did you hear about us?" The answer to that question cannot be trusted. People rarely know, care, or specifically remember how they FIRST heard about you.

This, too, is a relatively flawed system as you're relying on people to be 100% accurate when they often can't remember or just want to be polite and will say the first thing that pops into their head. Advertising is as much art as science or craft, and you should use these results with a grain of salt. Possibly two grains if you have them handy.

THE THREE KINDS OF THREE KINDS OF MEDIA

No, that's not a typo. As we help our own clients with media planning, we're radically rethinking how media works and how we make sure it works for us.

With so many media channels, you can really, really, REALLY burn through a METRIC TON of money quickly with little to no action or traction. How can you prevent that?

REFRAME THE WAY YOU THINK ABOUT MEDIA.

Now, several people—including me—have written about the *three* kinds of media: paid, owned, and earned.

BUT... the more we've been doing research for our clients and for this book, it's becoming pluperfectly clear to me that there are really *three kinds of three kinds* of media.

These are not independent silos; they're interdependent.

There's some overlap between them. It's not as though you need to have *nine* independent kinds of media. Rather, this is more of a construct for you to think about media in this day and age. When there are so many options. I think it makes it *simpler* to think of it in terms of three kinds of three kinds of media.

As you know, we believe strongly in The First Order of Business. It's a foundational approach to really reframe how you think about marketing holistically. Marketing for us is defined as "any interaction you have with a customer or a potential customer." That includes advertising where you dip into your pocket and spend. When we talk about media channels at the tip of the silo, I want you to think about it differently. In fact, you must! There have never been more channels, apps, and media opportunities available to you. If you're not careful, you could spread your money too thin or hoard too much of it. The result? You impair your efficiency, you waste money, and you don't reach your intended audience.

The Concentric Circle Media Planning Strategy

Let's look at a circle like this that goes inward.

The Three Kinds of Three Kinds of Media

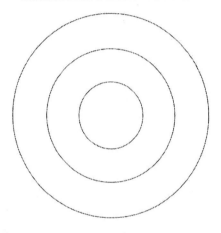

We'll start with the one most people know about.

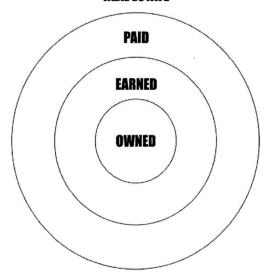

The Three Kinds of Three Kinds of Media
REAL ESTATE

PAID

EARNED

OWNED

We call the first concentric circle "Real Estate." Who owns it?

The outer circle is your paid media. That's where you reach into your pocket and pay a third party to run messaging.

The second circle inside Real Estate is earned media. Can you deliver an experience so good that people leave you reviews on Google, Yelp!, or Facebook? That people leave you reviews on ~~Angry's~~ Angie's List? That you get news media coverage because of something you're doing that's truly Shareworthy?

Then lastly, the inner circle is owned media. That is your own blog, your own website, and your content marketing strategy. You need to think about developing content that you own. We include media "rental" inside the ownership circle as well. You might hire a firm to help you get articles or whitepapers placed in front of the right people. If you're a marketer to car dealers doing business to business, and you can get a column on marketing placed in *Automotive News*, that's a really powerful placement for you.

Once I show you the other two concentric circles, you're going to see there is some overlap. Remember these are not mutually exclusive. These are not nine discreet silos. *It's simply a way to truly reframe the way you think about media planning, media buying, and media placement.*

Let's call our second circle "Term" – or the duration/length we plan to market a certain campaign.

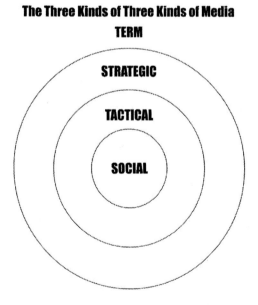

The Three Kinds of Three Kinds of Media
TERM

STRATEGIC

TACTICAL

SOCIAL

THE PURPOSE OF YOUR STRATEGIC MARKETING IS ALWAYS, ALWAYS, ALWAYS TO BE KNOWN, LIKED, AND TRUSTED BEFORE YOU'RE NEEDED.

When we buy broadcast media for our clients, it's typically for strategic purposes. We plan to be doing it as long as we plan to be in business. We continue to use radio very effectively for a lot of our clients. For some clients, we use television. For some clients, we use Facebook advertising. We know that we're going to be doing these things 52 weeks a year. The purpose of this marketing is to make consumers know, like, and trust our clients before that consumer's need arises.

The second circle of Term is tactical. Sometimes, whether it's a holiday, or something in your community, or just slow traffic, you need to turn a spigot to increase the flow of your message—that's tactical thinking. Seasons of the year and holidays are times when we see businesses become very tactical about their advertising. When you're doing media planning, you want to look at your calendar and see what themes arise and what windows might open where additional tactical marketing makes sense.

The third circle of Term is social. Social isn't up to you. Social is up to the masses. You never know who or when or what or why. You must always be mindful of your responsiveness, relevance, and your credibility when we're answering people's questions. When you, as Chris Brogan once said, "Grow bigger ears" to listen more acutely to what people are saying," you can help by having conversations with them.

Let's call the third concentric circle "Signal."

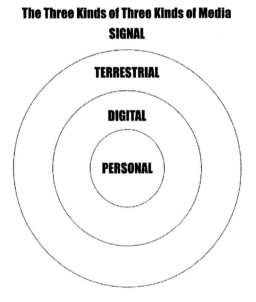

The Three Kinds of Three Kinds of Media
SIGNAL

TERRESTRIAL

DIGITAL

PERSONAL

Is it a terrestrial media form? Is it earth-based? What I mean by that is: Is it a media channel used before web browsing, scrolling, texting, tweeting, and twiddling our thumbs on our phones? Consider it similar to Charlemagne's distinctions between the eras Before Christ (B.C.) and Anno Domini (A.D.). We, too, could use something similar as in Before Digital (B.D.) and Era Cum Inter Se, Ut Solebat Attendere (era when we used to pay attention to one another... or E.C.I.S.U.S.A.).

Second is digital—which would include Facebook advertising, display advertising, re-targeting, pay-per-click advertising, marketing on LinkedIn or through YouTube pre-roll—anything that involves a computer, a mobile phone, an iPad, tablet, or other device is part of your digital strategy. Again, you may not buy all of these, but you want to make sure that when you're doing your yearly planning, you are thinking about all of these.

Then lastly is personal—what events are you going to sponsor? Are you going to any home shows? Are you going to have a Christmas open house at your place of business? What kind of cause marketing are you going to do? Are you going to contribute as a team to Habitat for Humanity? That counts for lost wages. That should be included in your marketing budget. Again, as you look at your marketing budget, I want you to think about all nine of these.

THE SPREADSHEET OF MEDIA AWESOMENESS

When we build a media plan for someone, we start with a blank spreadsheet tab. *NOTE: This is different from our media budget—which is a separate spreadsheet tab. A media/ marketing budget contains distinct, exclusive expenditures of money, time, or talent.* Our media **plan** will have overlap with channels in more than one cell, but that's necessary in our way of rethinking media to make sure we have all our bases covered.

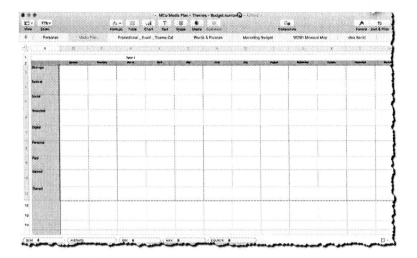

You can see in column A that we've got our three kinds of three kinds of media. Then your subsequent columns are your marketing windows. we've got the months across, those are our periods. Every business' windows may be different. You may have 13, 4-week windows. You may think quarterly. You may think every other week. Review pages 289-91 to think more deeply about how to properly spread out your calendar.

Is this a lot of work? Does it require a lot of thought?

Absolutely it does. If this was easy, everyone would be doing it. It's simple. It's simple to understand. If you're willing to do the work, you can boom your business and unleash your awesomeness on your market.

We think about it very differently because the world is very different. If you're not careful, you can waste and blow a lot of money really quickly. What we're advising you to do is just be more mindful about the fact that there's no longer one kind of media or even three kinds of media. Today in this Age of Rapid Distraction there are three kinds of three kinds of media.

How much should you spend for each?

How do you measure success of each?

What type of messaging works best for each?

Great questions. You're not only good-looking but smart, too.

Wait a minute... if I...

YES! YES! You've connected some magical dots!

IF YOU MERGE YOUR MEDIA PLAN WITH YOUR MESSAGE CALENDAR, YOU'VE GOT EVERYTHING YOU NEED TO CREATE MORE RELEVANT, CAPTIVATING MESSAGING MORE OFTEN.

Dude. I'm so proud of you!

"MURKY AT BEST..."

"We serve ads to consumers through a non-transparent media supply chain with spotty compliance to common standards, unreliable measurement, hidden rebates, and new inventions like bot and methbot fraud." -Marc Pritchard

Who's Marc Pritchard, you ask? Pritchard's the Chief Brand Officer of a little up and coming family business called... hold on, I have it here somewhere in my notes... oh! Yes! Here it is:

Procter & Gamble

Yes, *that* Procter & Gamble. The company famous for holding sacred the saying attributed to W. Edwards Deming: "In God we trust. All others bring data."

In an early 2017 speech to the Internet Advertising Bureau, Pritchard—giving one of the most important wakeup calls in recent advertising history—called digital advertising "murky at best and fraudulent at worst."

He explains: "Better advertising and media transparency are closely related. Why? Because better advertising requires time and money, yet we're all wasting way too much time and money on a media supply chain with poor standards adoption, too many players grading their own homework, too many hidden touches, and too many holes to allow criminals to rip us off."

Buyer Beware

When someone comes to you offering the next great shiny toy labeled as a solution, ask good questions:

- What independent monitoring organization verifies the data you're showing me?

- Can you provide sources for all your data?

- What's your role in this? Do you optimize and implement the technology or are you just an affiliate or reseller?

- Can you give me local references I can speak to about your successful partnership?

Pritchard sees the future for Procter & Gamble:

> *"Getting to a clean, productive media supply chain is the level playing field we all want and need. The basis for competitive advantage is our brands, our advertising craft, and the quality of our product and package experiences for consumers. It's not rocket science; it's really just common sense."*

I hope you see your future here, too. Your local media rep may not be dishonest as they pedal their latest, greatest wares. They may just be misinformed or ignorant... and, when it comes to your money, his ignorance will not lead to bliss.

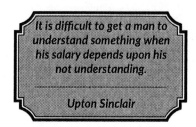

It is difficult to get a man to understand something when his salary depends upon his not understanding.

Upton Sinclair

HOW TO FREELY* AND QUICKLY GIVE YOURSELF** A SURPRISINGLY DECENT WORKING KNOWLEDGE OF ANY MEDIA CHANNEL***

The good news? Published material on any subject has never been more readily available at your fingertips.

The bad news? Published material on any subject has never been more readily available at your fingertips.

By using my technique below, you can develop enough knowledge about any media channel to decide (a) whether your team should use it, (b) how to optimize it, and (c) whether media vendors truly have your best interests—and those of your company—at heart.

We don't buy media for clients—though we have two vendors we trust implicitly if they do. And we regularly help clients evaluate media deals in any number of channels.

You, too, can use this technique.

Teach yourself how to use—or not use— any media channel:

You're going to use your favorite search engine to research a media channel. For purposes of this section, I'm going to use Google and research paid Facebook advertising.

Set your search limits to find only results published in the last year. While dozens of wonderful articles discuss proper Facebook advertising fundamentals from previous years, it's best to stick to sources accounting for the latest updates to Facebook. If you don't know how to do this, guess where you can learn? Google it!

Choose only organic search results—not paid. Nothing against the folks who pay Google to have their articles clicked, but we want those sources that other visitors have found naturally for two reasons:

1. The majority rules! People regularly found these articles for a reason, and that reason is most likely that the article contains relevant information.

2. The author rules! Chances are good the author, or the author's SEO firm, knows that Google rewards helpful information in a readable format. Those articles are most likely to show up at the top of Google's organic search engines. Your time is valuable. Leverage the fact the best internet writers know this.

Skim the first ten results for each search term below. Compile into either a binder or digital file. See what overlaps. See what patterns emerge. Put these in your notebook.

Here are your searches:

- Google "Facebook Advertising Dictionary/ Terminology" (many poor choices come simply from a lack of understanding of definitions of terms)

- Google "how to do great Facebook Advertising"

- Google "strange ways to advertise on Facebook"

- Google "Facebook advertising case studies"

- Google "Facebook advertising mistakes"

- Google "Facebook advertising pitfalls"

- Google "Facebook advertising myths"

- Google "everything you think you know about facebook advertising is wrong"

- Google "why you need to rethink your Facebook ad strategy"

- Google "best tools for FB advertising"

- Google "Facebook advertising FAQ"

- Google "how to pick a Facebook advertising company

- Google "[your industry] and Facebook"

After Google, go to YouTube (owned by Google) and do the same.

Do the companies listed in the search results have lead magnets (typically lists, charts, articles, infographics, or whitepapers available in exchange for an email address) related to your search? Use a Gmail address (not tied to your regular email) to sign up and download them.

You'll be amazed at just how few proper fundamentals there are to each media channel and how regularly those few fundamentals appear in each result.

Before long, you'll have a terrific brief on paid Facebook advertising! Well done!

* When I say freely, I'm referring to your financial budget. It will take some time.

** You can assign this to someone else on your team.

*** As you might suspect, this works with just about anything—not just media channels.

A PAID-MEDIA STRATEGY THAT'S WORKED FOR YEARS

This has worked for us in different countries and in different business categories for years, and I'm sharing it with you for the price of this book because I want to help. Most media buying firms will disagree with me. You know my feelings on most media buying firms, ad agencies, and grossly gross impressions and rating points.

Choose a broadcast medium that strategically suits you. For most of you, like most of our clients, the one that's going to reach the most people for the dollar is radio. Buy only stations you can afford to own. Don't be obsessed with the top-rated stations in your market. Remember to ask yourself: "How many customers do I need?" Typically, you can get better deals from stations lower on the proverbial food chain.

You are looking for cost per person per year. You want to shoot for no more than one dollar per person per year— meaning you want to pay no more than one dollar to reach a person three times a week every week for 52 weeks.

Do NOT buy weekly schedules or even 13-week schedules. Buy your radio one time per year. This will give you the greatest bulk discount and cost advantage.

Buy stations until you run out of money. If you can't afford to own stations with this formula of reaching listeners three times per week every week, buy a smaller section of the station using day-parts.

Plan to develop two to four new messages every month that are variations of the same core themes. The goal of your broadcast advertising schedule is to help position you as the company those listeners or viewers know, like, and trust when it comes time for them to need what you sell.

BUT I LIKE TV! Great! If TV has been working for you, keep using it. We have a client in a small, rural market who still buys both Yellow Pages and the local weekly community newspapers because they work. Every business is different. Every community is different. What's good for the goose is most certainly not always good for the gander. However, let me add a BUT of my own... when it comes to your long-term, brand-development media channel...

Resist the urge to run sales or promotions in your long-term media vehicle.

For this, you'll have a tactical second paid medium. Even in this day and age of digital, we prefer direct mail, but we do it differently than most people. Yes, you can—and should—use email, and you can also use Facebook for this and see a good response. We'll talk about both email and Facebook usage in upcoming chapters, but we prefer at least budgeting for and adding direct mail to this mix.

It's worth investing more in the product (paper) and doing your direct mail one of either two ways:

POSTCARDS: Think of the front of your postcard like a billboard. Use no more than eight words and an evocative picture. Make your offer clear and tied to your long-term brand position's values. Your offer's success will be tied to the credibility of your reason for lowering your prices.

HAND-WRITTEN CARDS: We get so few hand-written, hand-addressed pieces of mail with first-class stamps that they've become irresistible. These are particular good for reaching out to your current customer base to offer them something special. Maybe it's a sneak preview of new merchandise open only to them. Maybe it's a special "black card" that entitles them to members-only discounts. Maybe it's a party.

THE MYTH OF TRADITIONAL MEDIA MIX

I've had people argue, "Hey! AT&T does all kinds of media. Why shouldn't I?"

Because in 2016, according to Statista, McDonald's spent $1,460,000,000 in advertising. Do you plan on spending a billion and change? (Heck *their loose change* is $146,000,000.) If so, you might be able to afford to spread some around between different media.

Our clients have achieved success and growth by taking the opposite approach and dominating one advertising medium and, when budget allows, complementing it with a second medium that strategically fits our plan.

You're far more likely to be heard, seen, or read by being in the same place again and again and again.

I'm not going to tell you which media to choose. There are dozens of choices, and I'm unwilling to provide you with an oversimplified answer to a complicated, nuanced question.

It depends on your market and your competition and prices.

And, mostly, it depends on your messaging, your customer experience, your strategic plan, and your goals and values.

OWNED MEDIA: SEO 101

Simply put, the term "search engine optimization" refers to the following two-step process:

1.   Somebody goes to Google, Yahoo!, Bing, DuckDuckGo, or her search engine of choice and types in something.

2.   You show up... higher is better.

Is that simplified enough for you?

Now, you can pay thousands of firms thousands of dollars to help you rank higher for the terms of your choosing.

Not sure what those are? They can help you with that, too. Those terms can vary from the shortest, most obvious (and most competitive) terms to "long-tail" searches that involve, according to many studies, fewer searches but higher opportunities for conversion.

I'm going to tell you the one over-riding, timeless principle you should remember, and if you're a good, helpful company, should relax you when it comes to overwhelming world of SEO.

With each iteration of the search engines' algorithms (the formulas they use to help users get the right response to their queries), they're getting closer and closer to one truism:

Talk to people about what matters to people in a language they use and understand.

Got that? Sure, there are ways to optimize pages to help a little, but the main idea I want to you take away is that if you continue to be helpful and follow the other suggestions and fundamentals in this book, you will—over the long term—rise above your competition simply by being helpful.

With each passing hour, search engines want the same things customers want: honest answers from credible people.

COPYRIGHT & THE INTERNET

"You mean I can't just take this picture I found on Google and put it on my website?" "You mean I can't just take this web copy I liked from that website and put it on ours?"

No. You can't.

Understand, I'm not a lawyer.

But here's what I know for sure:

If YOU try and take our words, ideas, or other intellectual property WITHOUT my permission for your own commercial benefit, you will be hearing from my lawyer.

A good one. Educated at Oxford and everything. He wears cuff-links.

And my lawyer will tell you to not take other people's things without permission.

If you plead ignorance, cool. Copyright's a murky world, and I will probably go ahead and say "okay."

But you need my permission. As soon as I hit publish, I own the copyright. I don't need to put a little © thingie on it.

And you can't just save the poster image to your computer and photoshop out my friend's company logo and replace it with your own. The graphic designer owns that copyright.

Complicated? Yep.

And those images you take from Google? You don't own those.

But here's the great news!

There are a bazillion stock photo sites that allow you to buy rights to pictures. That's something you can Google.

Did you really think you could take stuff that wasn't yours without permission or credit?

What if you found somebody's taken your stuff?

Great question.

Here's our permissions policy if you're interested:

The (using-the-term-loosely) Intellectual Property (heretofore known as "stuff") Policies of Tim Miles.

Have a Hay Day: (use freely)

Post links to my website, TimMilesCo.com. Please.

Use stuff from my blog, books, and presentations under 200 words. The honor system applies here. And please give credit where credit is due—like "Tim Miles wrote this. He's kinda handsome. See more at TimMilesCo.com."

Copy my stuff if you're going to hand it out internally at your company, with let's say less than 50 copies. I'm cool with that so long as, again, you give credit where credit is due.

Whoa Nellie:

Get my permission before you:

Use stuff from my blog, books, and presentations to make money for yourself or others. This includes selling or licensing my content in printed or digital form, yo. This means on your website, apps, billboards, or pulling it behind a bi-plane.

Change anything I have written or produced to suit your purposes.

Put that horse back in the barn:

You may not, under any circumstances, repost my stuff in its entirety. Nor may you translate into other languages. I speak only English and a little igpay atinlay, and so I would lose creative control of my own stuff. That's not good. My son is learning Mandarin, but he just started. Give him a few years to master the language before you ask, okay?

I have business partners and family members who occasionally write for my blog or other projects. They own their own stuff and you'd better ask permission before you use that.

I don't get real serious very often. But my stuff is my life's work. It's my family's livelihood. It's proof to my mom that I have a real job. I need all the help I can get. I'm not the good son.

Follow these rules and we're good. Don't follow these rules ...

... and I've got an Oxford-educated attorney on speed dial who doles out million dollar big lawyery words like Chuck Norris doles out justice. Think the late Alan Rickman with a Juris Doctor.

BEING PRACTICALLY SOCIAL

> *"I don't use Twitter. It's not really me. I also don't actively use Facebook, and I'm not adding any friends. I don't want to use a tool unless I'm going to use it really well. Doing any of these things halfway is worse than not at all. People don't want a mediocre interaction." –Seth Godin*

It's very easy to get swept up in trying to do them all. It's intoxicating to belong and elicit response, but just like the idea of eating the triple-sasquatch-mega-burrito (with extra sour cream) seems awesome, you can't really finish... or even enjoy it.

The same is true with social media channels. You most likely can't choose them all.

Start simply: Choose one.

Pick a social media channel *you* enjoy. It might not even be the most popular one.

Don't worry about that. Pick one. Do it well. Study it. Take webinars about it. Learn as much as you can, and begin to use it expertly. Then, and only then, if you still have some energy, pick another that you like.

It's okay to pick ceramics, but if you do, I want you to become an expert in ceramics. I want you to learn as much as you can about doing it well, and you'll need to keep up with the rapidly changing ceramics technology. The good news is that it's never been easier, cheaper, or more convenient to learn. You should be able to teach others the basics quickly and clearly. You're going to be a master of ceramics.

And your company will be better for it.

IS THIS YOUR MOST VALUABLE EMPLOYEE?

She rarely misses an hour of work, much less a day. He's been known to be your best salesperson giving his best presentation on his very best day. She's a relationship deepener and wicked-awesome lead generator.

I'm talking, of course, about your website: your 24/7/365 help-desk, sales funnel, and customer relationship management tool that customers and customers-to-be can access from the privacy, comfort, and convenience of their own homes, phones, and offices.

As a part of your marketing plan, how important is your website and online presence?

I'm asking. At this point, I don't even care what your answer is as long as it's not, "I don't know."

Why?

Your website can be your best salesperson giving her very best presentation on her very best day.

Your website can be an interactive, full-color brochure for your company that I can enjoy in my underwear from the privacy, comfort, and convenience of my own home.

Your website can be an instant mobile portal to where you are and what I need and why I should come to where you are to get what I need.

Your content marketing and social media presence can be the best consumer research tool money doesn't have to buy.

Your content marketing and social media presence can be the best help desk money can buy, and it can help you drastically lower your advertising budget.

Because your website is at the hub of all you do online and frames the way many consumers perceive you offline, I want to make sure you're thinking about your website as you would any senior level employee.

Does your website have a job description?

Do you have a method of evaluating its job performance?

How often do you evaluate its performance?

Do you have a procedure in place for coworkers or customers to suggest improvements?

How much do you pay your website? In other words, how big is your budget for regular maintenance and improvement?

To give you an idea of how much we think about our clients' websites, we've put together both a 52-question online readiness test to help hammer home the idea of what a crucial role your website plays in your company. We follow that up with a simple maintenance checklist you—or someone you hire—should perform monthly (or at the beginning of each of the windows on your message calendar). We hope you find them helpful.

A 52-QUESTION ONLINE READINESS TEST

We came up with this list of questions about your company's presence on the web. We're curious if you have answers.

If you don't, does it bother you that you don't?

Let's consider these our baseline. We'll start building from here.

1.   If you're the owner, are you, or is your owner part of the web conversation? Does your online presence have his or her or your voice?

2.   How much time a week does your company spend thinking about and working on your web presence?

3.   When was the last time your website had a professional evaluation?

4.   Is your website the most important thing for your business' marketing?

5.   How much money do you have budgeted for website updates, optimization, content development, and security every month?

6. Is there a mobile version or at least a mobile-optimized landing page for your website? What's on it?

7. Have your website images been optimized for the web?

8. Are your images legal? Or did you just pull them off somebody else's site?

9. Did you know you couldn't do that?

10. If I want to get ahold of you, can I get ahold of you or find out how to get ahold of you on every page of your website? Is your phone number there? A contact link?

11. Is your phone number text so I could click on it from my mobile browser?

12. Do you have a job description for your website?

13. Do you have a method of measuring the success of your website?

14. Do you get analytics for your website? Do you know how to understand the analytics for your website?

15. Do you ever make any changes as a result of the analytics?

16. At the bottom of each page of your website, do you give me options, via links, where to go next?

17. Within about six seconds on your homepage can I tell what you do and how and why it affects me?

18. Do you have reviews on your website? How about testimonials? Is there a difference?

19. Written testimonials? Video testimonials?

20. Have you thought about font size on your website?

21. Do you own your Google My Business listing?

22. Do you know that Google recently switched up how you use your Google My Business listing?

23. Do you know what Google My Business is?

24. Do you know the second-most visited search engine on the web? Do you have a presence there?

25. Do you know everywhere customers can leave online reviews about your business?

26. Do you have a policy for monitoring those reviews?

27. Do you have a policy for replying to those reviews?

28. Do you use email marketing? Regularly?

29. Do you have a plan and policy for how often, to whom, and what you say in your email marketing?

30. Do you have any Google Alerts set up? Do you know why you should?

31. Do you use Twitter?

32. How do you use Twitter? Do you ever use Twitter to search or listen?

33. How about any of the location-based applications?

34. Do you have any videos on your site?

35. Where are they hosted?

36. Do you know what "hosted" means?

37. Do you have a blog? Is it updated? Do you know if it's been updated? Are you a contributor? Why not?

38. Remember those questions your business gets asked all the time on the phone? Do you have the answers to those questions on your website? Are the easily accessible and findable from the homepage? From the mobile landing page?

39. Do you have hyperlinks embedded into your copy to serve as touchpoints to deeper places within your website?

40. Can Google "see" your images? Do you have them properly formatted with alt tags?

41. Do you know the most important real estate on your website?

42. Do you know the most common size window people use to browse your website?

43. Does your website talk to the customer in the language of the customer about what matters to the customer? Or do you rely on jargon and self-serving statements?

44. Do you know what objections your customers regularly have? Does your website anticipate and overcome those objections?

45. Is your website easy to quickly scan? Does it make use of headings and subheadings and short paragraphs of text?

46. Do you know who's visiting your website?

47. Do you know what you want people to do on each page? Do you know what they need in order to feel comfortable doing what you want them to do on each page?

48. Do you use social media to engage with your customers, or do you use it as a megaphone to blast them with sales and other promotions? Or do you use it for both?

49. Do you send Facebook messages to your personal friends about your company? All of them at once? Telling them to like your page and not giving them a reason?

50. Do you use LinkedIn? How? Why?

51. Do you have a person on staff or an outside firm devoted to developing your web presence? Would you know what a job description for this person might look like? Would you know how to interview for this person?

52. When was the last time you used the Yellow Pages?

If you're freaked out right now, that's not necessarily a bad thing. This stuff is important. Hugely important. And not just for the Apples and the Ikeas and the Zapposeses of the world. But for you, too.

THE CHECKLIST FOR REGULAR WEBSITE MAINTENANCE

There are technical lists like this on the Internet for web developers, but we couldn't find one for owner-operators who update their sites themselves. So, this is our own non-technical checklist of stuff to consider updating a few times a year... starting now.

When was the last time you inventoried your website and made sure your content was fresh and appropriate?

If you're a small company who hasn't given much thought to your website since it was first built in 1997 or whenever, now's a good time to freshen it up.

I know you're busy, but this stuff matters, and you can use a change of seasons as your cue to remember to take a look.

1. Is your content seasonally appropriate? For example, we represent several heating & air conditioning companies, and we'll be telling them to make sure their air conditioner references are replaced with furnace and heat pump references. We'll have them inventory their images to make sure they show wintry stuff instead of sweltery stuff.

2. Check for outdated coupons, offers, and warranties.

3. Check for pictures of employees who are no longer with your company.

4. Add photos and bios of new employees.

5. Have a blog? When was your last post? If you're most recent post is more than a month old, either schedule several new ones or kill the blog until you have time to make it a priority (which you should totally do, by the way).

6. Have a news or media section? See #5.

7. Are your store or service hours listed? Will your hours change for holidays? Make a note NOW to update that on the appropriate day.

8. Do you use contact forms on your site? When was the last time you updated who gets those?

9. Speaking of which, do former employees still have access to the back-end of your site? Time to delete old users and possibly change passwords.

10. The same goes for your social media accounts. Check your admins.

11. Is you phone number at the top-right of every page? This should be an easy fix and you should do it right away.

12. A local company puts the picture of the person answering their phone on the contact page. I think that's brilliant.

13. Do all the links on your pages work? Check them.

14. Do you have any images that are slow to load? Optimize them for your website. Speed rules the web.

15. If you use pay-per-click advertising, have you checked to make sure your Adwords are updated and relevant? Is it time for a fresh landing page or two?

16. Check the mobile version of your site and make sure it formats appropriately and gives the info you want it to on the main page.

17. Make sure your copyright date on the site is current.

18. If you have social media buttons, make sure you've been social, or you just look bad. Make sure it's simple for people to share your info on social media as well.

19. Double-check phone, address, and email for everyone with contact info listed.

20. Freshen reviews, testimonials, and pull quotes. If you have them on your site, make sure the most recent one wasn't from three years ago.

Larger companies have staffs that should be doing these things on a daily or weekly basis, but we know it's harder for you when you wear so many hats.

You can save time by dividing up each main section of your site and assigning them to members of your staff. Have them go through each page looking for this checklist of things to update, delete, or improve.

Updating these things gives you credibility... Google will like your freshly updated, properly working, relevant content.

It can also be a 24/7 world-class help desk team providing solutions and helpful response to people in need. You wouldn't leave your best salesperson or your response team ill-prepared, would you?

THE 7 DEADLY SINS OF VIDEO

With the proliferation of affordable, available, high-speed Internet, video has taken over our phones, our tablets, our television, and our computers. Alongside this accessibility has come a decreased cost in production of your own videos for social media, content marketing, even television and YouTube preroll commercials.

That said, please use caution when producing your own videos. Yes, you can do them for a fraction of what production cost even five years ago, but also yes, they can easily look and sound worse than even five years ago.

Poor quality video (or any marketing for that matter) hurts your credibility, and we—as an audience—are judging you by your technical proficiency whether consciously or not.

The Internet (particularly YouTube) is filled with wonderful resources to not only tell but show you how to make better videos, but in the meantime, here are the heavy seven:

1. Poor stability

You can purchase a small tripod at the nearest convenience store. Do so and lock down your phone or camera. If you're shooting external or internal motion, purchase a gimbal for your phone that contains gyroscopes to keep its pans and tilts smooth and steady. Yes! Your phone is fine.

2. Letting someone talk you into believing you need an expensive camera

Sure, it'd be nice to shoot in 360-degree, 8k resolution, BUT YOU HAVE NO REASON—YET—TO DO SO TO TELL YOUR STORY. Most cell phones now allow you to shoot as high as 4k resolution, but as I type this, 1080p resolution will serve you well.

3. Poor lighting

People are shocked when we show up to record video using our phone, but that's not all we show up with... we show up with a three-point lighting kit to make sure our subject is well lit. With a little bit of online research, you'll have no trouble finding inexpensive, helpful lighting.

4. Poor sound

You must, must, MUST purchase an external microphone to capture the authentic warmth of the human voice.

5. Poor (or lack of) editing

Even phones, iPads, and your personal laptop have simple video/audio editing programs to clean up, trim, tighten, and lighten your videos. Once you have our interest, keep it by keeping us on our toes.

6. Using only one long, static shot

Learn a little about in-frame editing, panned still shots, B-roll, stock video, titles, intros, lower-thirds. The internet has a vast wealth of knowledge to help you keep our interest as we watch.

7. Not having a plan before you press record

Huh? What were all those things you just said? Well, when you plan to incorporate video into your media strategy, you should plan to learn each of these concepts and their rules for substance and style usage.

Please, don't just wing it. You'll fall flat.

THE 10 COMMANDMENTS OF EMAIL

Reports of email's demise have been greatly exaggerated.

Did you know, for example, that 91% of people check their email at least once per day?

Did you know, for example, that 44% of email recipients made a purchase in the last year based on a promotional email?

Email's evolved, certainly, but that doesn't mean you can't evolve along with it. In fact, by working through this book, you're well-positioned to take advantage of this remarkably effective channel.

There are countless books, articles, videos, and tutorials about how to get greater impact from your email. In the meantime, here are ten unwavering principles.

1. Thou Shalt Not Send Email Without Permission

Don't buy a list, don't send to your Facebook friends, don't take emails from business cards and send bulk emails. It's illegal, and it repels the very people you're trying to attract.

2. Thou Shalt Make Sure Emails Are Properly Formatted For Mobile

The greatest evolution in email (besides perhaps advanced spam filtering) is that we're no longer simply receiving it in Outlook on our desktop PC. These days, most major email services will not only help you auto-format, but will also let you test your email and its appearance in various browsers, devices, and email applications.

3. Thou Shalt Use A Major Email Marketing Company

Yes, they cost a little, but when you factor in cost-per-lead, email marketing is still one of the most efficient uses of your marketing budget. Legitimate email marketing companies do the heavy lifting of sorting lists, doing their best to ensure compliance (and keeping you out of spam folders), and providing you detailed analytics so you can measure success.

4. Thou Shalt Measure Success

What's the point of email marketing if you're not looking at the results of your campaigns? Make a plan to study the analytics of a campaign 72 hours after its launch. What can you learn? What follow-up actions can you take? What should you try differently?

5. Thou Shalt A/B Test

Why not test two different subject lines? Leave the email entirely the same but test two different headlines and see if there's a marked difference in results between the two? Or why not test two different calls-to-action? By regularly testing ONE THING AT A TIME (thus, A/B), you'll begin to learn what actually works instead of merely guessing what you think should work.

6. Thou Shalt Properly Size And Format Images

Size matters when it comes to emails because speed matters. Your large picture needs to be optimized so it loads quickly. Luckily, that's one of the many benefits of using a major email marketing company - they'll help you with such things. Also, make sure you fill out the [alt tag] information. What's that? Well, many email applications don't show images by default unless a user specifically requests to load them. Until they're loaded, the email viewer will at least see whatever you type as the [alt tag].

7. Thou Shalt Study Subject Line Writing

Google "How to write better email subject lines." You'll get approximately 837,000 responses. Read every article on the first three pages of the search results. Take good notes. Practice.

8. Thou Shalt Make It Clear What You Want Your Reader To Do Next

Have clear calls-to-action. What is it, specifically, you want your reader to do because of your email? This is a great thing to A/B test.

9. Thou Shalt Continue The Scent Trail On The Web

Does your call-to-action hyperlink back to your website? Make sure the same picture and language you used in your email are on that target (or landing) page on your website. Make sure your reader has confidence they're at the right place.

10. Thou Shalt Follow Our RACES & CARS Formula

Stick to relevance, authenticity, captivation, elephant, social proof, clarity, action, results, and additional social proof along with these other nine commandments, and you'll be ahead of the game when it comes to opt-in email marketing.

WHEN SHOULD YOU INVITE YOUR CLIENTS VIA EMAIL?

This is an email sent to Robert Earl Keen's email list on September 14th, 2014, which is the late President Taft's birthday. He was our largest U.S. President, and Keen decided to use the occasion to put all XXL sizes and larger on sale for 40% off! Genius!

It follows one of our golden rules for when to hold/send email and direct mail promotion:

Find unusual-but-relevant reasons to celebrate. Here, Keen is tying the message/promotion to an unusual theme.

This has two direct and immediate benefits:

You won't be emailing the same day as everybody else.

Your email will captivate people—instantly passing through the gatekeeper in their brains on the lookout for boring, irrelevant stuff—but it will still have an impact because it's not just weird, but weird AND relevant.

Tons of companies celebrate President's Day with promotions. Everyone celebrates Black Friday with promotions. (And NO ONE should celebrate certain days with certain kinds of promotions).

Look through the calendar... Google "unusual events in October" or "silly holidays."

Brainstorm with your team on how to tie-in promotions to those holidays. If you're a pizza place, maybe you celebrate the signing of the International Cheese Treaty.

If you're a creative company, maybe you close on Jim Henson's birthday.

If you're an ice cream or fro-yo place, maybe you give away free cones on the first day of Spring.

Conventional wisdom tells most companies to send out email "newsletters" on the first Tuesday, Wednesday, or Thursday of each month.

Why? Don't you agree that conventional wisdom tends to be more convention than actual wisdom?

Avoid emailing when everyone else does.

Find unusual-but-relevant reasons. Make them either relevant to your industry (Groundhog Day for a heating and air company, for example) or your promotion.

LAST BUT MOST CERTAINLY NOT LEAST: COMMUNITY MARKETING

In addition to budgeting time for your people to volunteer, we always encourage our clients to support their community, but one way we may differ is that our counsel includes the phrase: "Presence... not just presents."

Sure, it's fine to spend a hundred (or a few hundred) on a high school football sign, but we look for ways to make sure our team can get out and participate in Relays for Life or golf outings or sponsor Easter egg hunts.

If one of your employees comes to you and asks about sponsoring his daughter's softball team, and you have the budget for it, by all means do it, but also make sure you have enough to spring for the juice boxes and treats after the games. Spend a little extra and get matching t-shirts/jerseys for the parents. Make it fun. Make it fit your core values.

Family businesses have a responsibility to the communities they serve. Find ways to serve them. Budget generously for them. You'll be glad you did.

THIS BEARS REPEATING ABOUT MEDIA

The number of channels—a.k.a. the number of places to spend your budget—is growing by the day, and you have to be wary about the agenda and self-interest of those who tell you their channel is perfect for you.

Remember, if you've worked diligently on the other four tiers of The First Order of Business, then you're prepared to harness the power of any channel as best you can.

Can it be tricky? Absolutely. That's why our company works so hard with our clients to focus on the first four foundational tiers and works pro-actively on a message calendar and thinks long-term. It lets media representatives bring their best deals to us, and because we're prepared, it lets us walk away from anything that doesn't appear like a good value.

We hope these fundamentals have helped give you a solid understanding of how media works, and that there are no easy answers when it comes to channel choices (heck, three more hot new places to spend your money have probably popped up in the time it took me to type this paragraph).

THAT CONCLUDES OUR STUDY OF THE FRAMEWORK WE CALL THE FIRST ORDER OF BUSINESS.

WE'RE ALMOST HOME! WE HAVE JUST A FEW SIMPLE, INSPIRATIONAL IDEAS TO HELP YOU TAKE ACTION.

"Never turn your back on a weasel with a calculator."

-Roy H. Williams

> Were you put on this earth to be a painter, a scientist, an apostle of peace? In the end, that question can only be answered by action.
>
> Do it or don't do it.

STEVEN PRESSFIELD

March 2016

SECTION SIX

MEDIA

MESSAGING

CUSTOMER EXPERIENCE

STRATEGIC PLANNING

GOALS AND VALUES

TAKING ACTION

NO TIME TO WORK ON YOUR BUSINESS?

Schedule it! Now!

But... but... but...

I hear you, and I used to be like you, but our company began to improve exponentially when we scheduled one day at the end of each quarter and two days at the end of each year to put aside the day-to-day urgencies to fly up to 30,000 feet and focus on the important decisions, ideas, plans, and action steps to intentionally take this company where we want it to go.

You say you can't afford the time? I say you can't afford not to make the time, and in making this time and following through on quarterly company retreats, you'll soon find you had the time open and available thanks to these meetings.

11 TIPS FOR A BETTER COMPANY RETREAT

1. HAVE ONE

You think you're just too busy to have a retreat? So does everyone. Schedule it. Make one of the goals of your retreat to analyze why you don't think you have the time to have one.

2. KEEP AN ONGOING AGENDA

You never know when inspiration is going to strike. Start a shared file somewhere immediately where people can add agenda items year-round as they think of them. If you're a large company, you may want to choose to exclude some of them, but be sure to tell whomever includes it why you made your choice.

3. CHUNKS

Schedule related items in chunks with nice breaks in between. For example, in one chunk we talked strictly about clients—current, prospective, and what we think our ideal clients' (and disaster clients') personas would be. Another session was about HR, another was about our own marketing plan and its subtopics.

4. BREAKS

Schedule healthy breaks for email checking and phone calls and decompressing and plain ole' interstitial time for people to chat with each other.

5. RESPECT

During the chunks, keep your phones off and email closed. Respect the chunks and breaks.

6. MEALS

Cater extensively. Go out together. Share long (scheduled) meals. Get the introverts out but then be sure to schedule time for them to recharge.

7. ROLES

These jobs can rotate, but someone should take notes. Someone should make sure things keep moving. Someone should—SQUIRREL!

8. PARKING LOT

Someone should mind the parking lot. When things start to veer off-topic, feel free to say "parking lot" (or call out the aforementioned rodent). Whoever minds the parking lot writes down (parks) the intruding topic for later discussion before the retreat ends.

9. CLEAN UP THE PARKING LOT

Make time at the end to address the squirrel topics. Are they worthy of this retreat? If not, schedule someone to do something with each one for follow-up. (See more details in the next chapter.)

10 REVIEW

This is the most important part. What have you learned? What will you do differently as a result of this retreat?

11. FOLLOW THROUGH

No. Wait. This is the most important part. What are your action steps? What must be done?

TAKING ACTION

THE POWER OF THE WEEKLY REVIEW

What did you do this week? Can you tell me? How about your team and those action steps toward your goals, toward your vision? Did who get what done by when?

With life moving so fast and so much news and data pelting us in the face, it's getting harder and harder to remember what we did yesterday, much less Monday.

And if we can't remember what we did, how can we know where we're headed with any degree of certainty?

That's why weekly reviews rock.

Take some time every Friday (or Sunday evening), and look back on what you've done.

Review your sent items folder in your email.

Review your project management software (we're using, and loving, Trello). Are there any malignant tasks infecting your to-do list? Do them, delegate them or delete them.

Review the meetings you held and the phone calls you took. Did you get down all the necessary next steps?

Review the notes you took and the stuff you highlighted in the books you're reading.

Review your big picture goals. Did you make any small steps towards them this week?

There's still time—today.

Reviewing this week helps give it closure and give you confidence that you're pointed in the right direction come Monday.

If you do a 30-60 minute review of the week behind you, then you can put it behind you, enjoy your weekend, and move forward fiercely next week.

One last reminder: Reviews work only if they include reflection, refinement, and response.

Your productivity muscles may be sore at first, but you can do this!

THE IMPACT OF SIMPLE SEQUENCING

How do you benefit as a company from a great brainstorming session?

Let's say you got the gang all together. You gave them an email with the agenda a few days ahead of time so all the deep introverts in the group had time to think. You set the parameters for the quest and kept a positive, no criticism environment. The brainstorming session couldn't have gone better and now you have a white board packed with ideas. What's next? How does your business get better as a result?

The answer is in sequencing—a concrete sequence of events that will accomplish that idea.

Let's say you've all agreed on one idea that came out of the brainstorming session. You are convinced it will positively influence your bottom line and your employees are excited about the idea.

It may have five steps or 500 steps, but you will never get there unless you identify the steps, plan the journey, and get started.

1. Identify the target date for implementing the big idea.

2. Identify every step necessary, down to the most infinitesimal detail, necessary to implement said big idea.

3. The last shall be first! When sequencing the steps, work *backwards* from the completed task to the first step that needs taken. You may want to use index cards or sticky notes for this part because this usually takes a little rearranging.

4. Identify how much time each task will take and who will be responsible for accomplishing.

5. Check your time-line and adjust your completion date accordingly. If you have plenty of time, then identify the start date for the first task.

6. Go! Work the plan.

7. Set regular check-ins with everybody involved. Don't micromanage along the way, but be sure everyone knows what is expected and when it is expected from the get-go.

8. Adjust the timeline after each check-in.

9. Launch your idea.

10. Evaluate the process. Discuss with each participant and review timeline. This will not only improve your process for the next great idea, but will also affirm employees in the process.

This approach becomes more complex, depending on the goal, but it helps you layout a specific tactic for accomplishing a great idea. I've used it for everything from planning a kid's birthday party to communication strategies for a school district with 18 campuses.

Next time you decide to implement a great idea, try simple sequencing.

Otherwise, all those great ideas? They might just stay on the white board.

THE DIET & EXERCISE OF MARKETING

In marketing and advertising, like diet and exercise, you have to:

1. Start. Not tomorrow. Not next week. Now. Stop waiting for the "right time." It doesn't exist.

2. Do the work. It's exhausting. It's traumatic. It's terribly awkward. If it were easy, everyone would do it.

3. Hire a professional who can identify your weakness, establish a regimen, get your butt in gear, and push you kicking and screaming outside of your comfort zone. This is essential. If you try to do it alone, you simply won't do it.

4. Stick with it. Be tenacious. Force yourself to do it every day. Doing it only once a month won't get you anywhere.

5. Stop looking for magic pills or gimmicks. They don't exist. Those who claim they do are out to hurt you.

6. Expect setbacks and plateaus. They're inevitable. Prepare to ride out the storm when your continued efforts aren't producing the expected results. Refine your efforts.

7. Celebrate victories. Especially the small ones. They make up the big ones.

8. Repeat steps 1-7.

Remember, the definition of insanity is doing the same thing over and over and expecting new results.

EIGHT CELEBRATIONS YOUR COMPANY SHOULD HAVE

What do you celebrate? We firmly believe that celebrations belong in business. You need to strive to keep your employees as happy as you want your customers to be.

Celebrate their milestones. Celebrate their accomplishments. Celebrate when they represent the goals and values of your organization.

Here are some happenings we think worthy of celebration:

1. "What a Week!"

Any time an employee exhibits extreme tenacity through a tough work week, present them with a traveling trophy engraved "What a Week!" Let them pass it on to the next guy, encouraging and observing the hard work of others in the company.

2. "Called Out"

When a customer compliments one of your employees by name, present them with a $25 gift card. This encourages employees to make sure the customer knows their names. Which is also helpful on the rare occasion things don't go so well.

3. "Extra Mile"

On days when an employee goes the the extra mile, write a note that simply says, "We noticed," or buy them lunch. Employees of a local contractor working on Friday were treated to lunch by the VP of the company. He delivered it to the work site and expressed appreciation for their hard work, going the extra mile to meet a deadline on a day that everyone else had off for the long holiday weekend. By the way, he was working too, which added to their appreciation and his credibility.

4. "Sherlock"

Reward employees for solving customer problems, whether real or perceived. Leaving on a Friday is a tremendously motivating reward, especially in the summer. Recently, a president and CEO we know of a $3+ million dollar organization manned the phones all afternoon so her employees could enjoy a longer weekend. We love that kind of servant leadership! Plus, it was a great opportunity for the president to get back into the trenches and listen to real customer challenges.

5. "Thankfully You Rock"

Celebrate gratitude. At Thanksgiving, or any time of the year.

6. "Meanwhile..."

Acknowledge employee accomplishments outside the workplace.

7. "So Random!"

Promote and reward random acts of kindness.

8. "Give a Little Bit"

Support your employees charitable contributions and volunteerism. Consider an employee match for donations, or schedule a company work day at the volunteer event your employee is organizing.

What you celebrate teaches you (and us) a lot about your company. What do you celebrate? How do you celebrate? Every day, in big and small ways, celebrate the VIP customers of your business or organization—your employees.

STRATEGIC DOING MADE SIMPLE

The leaders at Ryan's church asked members for feedback. They were each given two simple questions to answer about specific areas of the church building:

What are we doing right? Where can we improve?

They received 337 comments. Forty percent praised what the church was doing well, and around 60 percent suggested ways to make it better.

Now, here's what the average North American church would do with this data:

- Form a "Suggestions Committee" to read, edit, pare down, and collate the findings.

- The committee chairperson would formally present their findings to the deacons.

- The deacons would add the discussion to next month's deacon's meeting.

- At next month's meeting, the deacons would pore over the data and determine that only a handful of the 337 comments should be considered.

- These comments would then be passed on to the Feasibility Committee to determine if they were doable.

- After identifying only three suggestions as feasible, the Feasibility Committee then passes those three findings on to the Finance Committee to find out whether there is money in the budget to cover the cost of implementation.

- Once approved by the Finance Committee, the deacons call a special church business meeting.

- The suggestions are brought before the church body.

- The church body would offer their thoughts and concerns.

- The church body would then vote on the proposed suggestions.

- The vote passes... maybe.

- The suggestions are then disseminated among the various church committees who may or may not take action.

Yep, that's what the average church would do, but this is not the average church.

No committees. No meetings. No vote. They simply started making changes.

"We need parking spots for expectant mothers."

Boom. Done.

"The foyer needs better directional signs to specific areas."

Boom. Installed.

"It would be nice to have name tags and lanyards for volunteers and greeters."

Boom. Laminated.

"The walls of the worship center need a new color scheme."

Boom. Painted.

They took the suggestions and ran with them. The church building has improved. So has morale among members because the church leaders have demonstrated that ideas are not only welcome but essential.

What about you? Are you willing to ask your employees or your customers for their input? More importantly, are you willing to follow-through and implement some of their ideas?

Begin with these two questions:

1. What are we doing well?

2. Where can we improve?

You need to be prepared for some bonehead answers and not-so-constructive criticism. But you also need to be prepared for some jaw-dropping, mind-blowing, why-didn't-I-think-of-that-myself ideas.

Then, execute. Apply. Make it so. Just don't form a committee.

As American inventor and industrialist Charles F. Kettering wisely noted, "If you want to kill any idea in the world today, get a committee working on it."

FINALLY

Be frequent. Be consistent. Be relevant.

Wait. Isn't that how we started this book??? And weren't those very techniques—used to create a conditioned response in 1904—awarded a Nobel Prize??? Maybe everything isn't so different now, but also maybe we had to work hard to learn you have everything you need inside you.

Yep: To modernize your marketing, you must first look *inward!*

Wow, we've come a long way since then, and if you've finished this book, you have, too.

Relax... you've got this. If you have questions, we'll be hosting webinars, classes, and providing volumes of free information and helpful tactics in articles and videos at BrandYourOwn.Business.

Congratulations. Now, get to work!

—THE END—

To order the full-size, comprehensive *Brand Your Own Business* workbook with exercises and in-depth additional content in each section, visit:

www.BrandYourOwn.Business

ABOUT THE AUTHORS

About Tim Miles

For nearly a quarter century, Tim's been writing about stuff he finds interesting and hoping people find it helpful. He's Head Custodian for a weird little marketing and management consulting firm. He's a recovering golfer and can probably beat you at Galaga. Tim and his family live in Franklin, Tennessee.

About Ryan Patrick

Born and raised in southern Illinois, Ryan spent most of his childhood recording silly voices and mindless musings into his tape recorder. Not much has changed except, now, he gets paid to do it. Ryan's a copywriter, producer, speaker, husband, father, actor, reader, autograph collector, M*A*S*H fan, and lover of cheese. He's also a partner with the Wizard of Ads group and Grand Poo-bah of Message Development for Tim Miles & Co.

About Lynn Miles Peisker

Lynn Miles Peisker manages projects in the Marketing Communications division at the University of Notre Dame. For years, she kept the plates spinning at Tim Miles & Company, and before that worked in education and non-profit sector communication strategy. She loves sorting everything from socks to ideas, and feels optimism and empathy are essential to success. She and her husband, John, and their dog, Poppy, live in South Bend, Indiana.

Tim Miles would like to thank:

Roy Williams for being such a wonderfully wise man, Will & Sarah Miles, John Miles, Pennie Williams, Corrine Taylor, Jeffrey & Bryan Eisenberg, Erin Richardson, Steve Rae, Adam Donmoyer, Jeff Sexton, Michele Miller, Paul Boomer, Ray Seggern and all my partners in Wizard of Ads®, Nancy Schneider, Mark & Bethany Dynis, Reis, Joey, Scotty, Bremer, Welker, Falcone, Seiters, the Zimmer brothers, my second family at D. Rowe's, my weird third cousins at Shakespeare's Pizza, Claire and all The Frothy Monkeys in Franklin, all our clients, and most of all: my families in Gifford, Centerville, and here in Franklin. Y'all—most notably Deidre—deserve to be co-authors of this book.

Ryan Patrick would like to thank:

My lovely wife, Julie, for being the most patient and understanding woman on earth; my kids, Rylie & Charlie, for giving me gray hairs to make me look more distinguished; Tim & Deidre Miles for giving me a chance to do what I sometimes excel at doing, Lynn Peisker for being the older sister I never had, my family—Mom, Dad, Reggie, Judy, Jean & Jo, and Carrie Waller—I love you all. Thanks also to Pat, Kent, Tracy, Miller, Laura & Mallory, my theatre gang, the Awesome Hometeam®, John A. Logan College, Steve Martin, Aaron Sorkin, Neil Simon, Larry Gelbart, and Jack Benny. Ryan would also like to thank 92% of the people Tim thanked.

Lynn Miles Peisker would like to thank:

All those who help me learn the gracious art of communication based on goals and values, especially Tim and Ryan.

ABOUT TIM MILES & Co.

Who We Can Help:

The clients we serve range from home services to medical to nonprofit to dry powder storage custom sheet metal fabrication. Oh, and we help sell swimwear to Canadians. Isn't that weird?

We also give away most of our stuff for free: We write, we podcast, and we speak to help non-client family businesses or nonprofits. We also speak to and train Fortune 500 corporations.

What We Do for Clients:

We help our clients in every facet of their marketing using this very First Order of Business methodology. It's a holistic approach that includes goal-setting, values-uncovery, strategic planning, customer experience, employee engagement, message development, and media planning and placement for the three kinds of three kinds of media.

Speaking / Webinars / Workshops:

We'd be happy to speak at your conference, convention, company, or college about a wide range of topics. We're received standing ovations from groups as large as McDonald's Corporation and as small as the most passionate six-person nonprofit organization you'll ever meet.

The only size that matters is the size of your heart.... not your P & L. If you think that sounds kinda weird, we agree. But we think it's a good weird, don't you?

-CONTACT INFORMATION-

WEBSITES:

WWW.TIMMILESCO.COM

WWW.BRANDYOUROWNBUSINESS.COM

FUNNYBUSINESSPODCAST.COM

CONTACT:

WWW.TIMMILESCO.COM/CONTACT

(615) 538-5511

SPEAKING, WEBINARS & WORKSHOPS

WWW.TIMMILESTALKS.COM

MANAGEMENT & MARKETING CONSULTING

WWW.TIMMILESHELPS.COM

LOVE LETTERS & HATE MAIL

tim@timmilesco.com

Tim Miles & Company

188 Front Street, Suite 116-19

Franklin, TN 37064